THE IRISH COLLEGE AT SANTIAGO DE COMPOSTELA

THE IRISH COLLEGE AT SANTIAGO DE COMPOSTELA

1605–1769

Patricia O Connell

FOUR COURTS PRESS

Typeset in 11 pt on 13.5 pt AGaramond by
Carrigboy Typesetting Services, County Cork for
FOUR COURTS PRESS LTD
7 Malpas Street, Dublin 8, Ireland
e-mail: info@four-courts-press.ie
and in North America for
FOUR COURTS PRESS
c/o ISBS, 920 NE 58th Avenue, Suite 300, Portland, OR 97213.

A catalogue record for this title is available
from the British Library.

10–digit ISBN 1–84682–032–4
13–digit ISBN 978–1–84682–032–8

Printed in England
by Antony Rowe Ltd, Chippenham, Wilts.

Contents

To the memory of the *seminaristas* of the
Irish College in Santiago de Compostela

One needs an adequate account of the wandering priests and friars moving hither and thither between this country and the continent, suffering so deeply, striving so gallantly to keep the institutional side of the Church from utterly fading away.

Daniel Corkery, The Hidden Ireland

Preface

About ten years ago I started on a series of studies of the six Irish Colleges founded in the Iberian peninsula between the years 1590 and 1649. This is the third volume in the series and follows *The Irish College at Alcalá de Henares, 1649–1785*, published in 1997, and *The Irish College at Lisbon, 1590–1834*, published in 2001.

The colleges were founded chronologically as follows:

> Lisbon 1590
> Salamanca 1592
> Santiago de Compostela 1605
> Seville 1608 or 1612
> Madrid 1629
> Alcalá de Henares 1649

Perhaps a chronological publication of the series would have been the most logical one. However, I make no apology for the eccentricity of my choice of publication order which is based on many outside factors. My next venture will be the daunting one of charting the history of the jewel-in-the-crown, 'el real colegio de S. Patricio de nobles irlandeses', the Irish College at Salamanca, in the illustrious and ancient university city on the Tormes.

Although I have visited the beautiful city of Salamanca several times, my most recent trip there in November 2004 was the high-point for me. So much has happened in the last few years to this city (its university founded in the early thirteeenth century), formerly neglected and in the doldrums due to the downgrading of its colleges since the nineteenth century, when this unique seat of learning was practically closed down, followed by decades of neglect and sterility. It has now blossomed out of all recognition in the new forward-looking Spain which has found again the confidence and spirit of its *siglo de oro* – the golden age of Spanish culture. An added delight for me was that I went back to Salamanca with a group of forward-looking, confident, mostly young, Irish academics from the four corners of Ireland to attend an International Symposium on Spanish-Irish Relations through the Ages. It was a glorious return of the Irish to their old stomping ground, and scholarly papers on a wide variety of subjects, academic, commercial, political and spiritual were contributed by both Irish and Spanish scholars. It opened a window on the many Spanish academics who are now currently taking a more than passing interest in the contribution of the Irish emigrés to Spanish life. There is now a proliferation of learned works on the history of the Irish in Spain since the seventeenth century. The future of Irish-Spanish studies is in good hands and is looking very healthy indeed. Furthermore we were lodged in the former Irish College for the duration of the seminar, which has now been refurbished in the most tasteful and comfortable way as part of the university. A far cry from the dejected and neglected college of former times.

In the writing of this present volume on the Irish College in Santiago de Compostela I have been deeply indebted to many librarians, archivists and historians for their unstinted help and cooperation. I wish to particularly thank my friend, Agnes Neligan, librarian in NUI Maynooth, for originally inviting me to look at the Salamanca Archives which had been deposited in the Russell Library in Maynooth many years before, in the 1950s, when the last Irish College in Spain closed down and its archival treasures came back to Ireland. Only a small number of scholars had made use of this unique resource since then and I very much appreciated the honour she conferred on me in inviting me to view the wondrous world of original manuscripts almost totally in sixteenth and seventeenth century Spanish (but also including later material) which made up this magnificent collection. I am glad to say that things have changed considerably in recent years. My degree of MA, for which I studied in UCD, now NUI Dublin, was primarily in Spanish literature but as it happens when I joined the staff of the Department of Spanish and Italian there I was also engaged in the study of manuscript material from Spanish archives which was a valuable experience and involved me in the study of paleography in relation to Spanish manuscripts.

I must also acknowledge with much gratitude the help, friendship, expertise and encouragement of the library staff in the NUI Maynooth and especially Penny Woods and Paul Hoary and many others in the Russell Library and Dr Tom O'Connor, History Department, NUI Maynooth, a friend of long standing, for generous help and advice. I am most grateful to Dr Declan Downey, History Department, NUI Dublin for reading my final draft and for making comments and suggestions which were very helpful. I am also appreciative of his constant interest and valued friendship.

Dr Fergus O'Donoghue SJ, scholar, archivist, historian and editor has kindly allowed me access to the valuable collections of Jesuit papers in the Jesuit Archives, Dublin, and I am very grateful to him for his help and advice regarding the available documents. I am also grateful for the reference facilities in the libraries of Mater Dei Institute, Dublin and the James Hardiman Library, NUI Galway on occasions.

The continued interest of successive Spanish ambassadors in Dublin, including Don José de Carvajal, has been of immense satisfaction and very welcome. In addition, I have to say a special word of thanks to my dear friend, Laura Miranda de Lennon, the ever-helpful and charming secretary of the Ambassador of Spain, for advice and aid way beyond the call of duty. For her interest, enthusiasm and invaluable insights I have also to mention my appreciation of the former Education Technical Advisor at the Spanish Embassy, Rosa López Boullón de Daly, now back living near the glorious city of Santiago de Compostela in her native Galicia, but still a frequent visitor to our shores and a true friend of Ireland.

Lastly my heartfelt thanks are due to family members, Maura, Annette, John and Nicholas in particular, to Maura for critical readings of endless drafts and Nicholas for sharing his expertise in computer science on many crucial occasions. Needless to say, I am eternally grateful to Michael Adams and his staff for their publishing skills.

Abbreviations

Arch. Hib.	*Archivium Hibernicum*
Arnáiz-Sancho	María-José Arnáiz and José-Luís Sancho, *El colegio de los irlandeses* (Alcalá de Henares, 1985)
AR	Annual Report
BHS	*Bulletin of Hispanic Studies*
BHS of Portugal	British Historical Society of Portugal
Coll. Hib.	*Collectanea Hibernica*
Couselo	José Couselo Bouzas, *El colegio de irlandeses de Santiago de Compostela* (Santiago, 1935)
CRS	Catholic Record Society
f.	folio
ff	folios
IER	*Irish Ecclesiastical Record*
Knights	Micheline Kerney Walsh, *Spanish Knights of Irish Origin*, 4 volumes (Dublin 1960–78)
mrs	*maravedís*
NUI	National University of Ireland
O'Doherty	Rev. Denis O'Doherty, series of articles in *Arch. Hib.* 2–4 (1913–15)
rrs	*reales*
Rep. Novum	*Reportorium Novum*
RIA	Royal Irish Academy
Rivera	E. Rivera Vázquez, *Galicia y los jesuitas: sus colegios y enseñana en los siglos XVI al XVIII* (Santiago, 1989)
Sal. Arch.	Salamanca Archives, NUI Maynooth [citation form changes from vol. 34 forword]
v.	verso or volume
Sea. AM	*Seanchas Ard Mhaca*, journal of the Armagh Diocesan Historical Society

Glossary of Spanish Words

alcabala	sales tax
alimentos	food or maintenance
arroba	an old Spanish weight, about 25 lbs; it was also a liquid measure
ayuntamiento	municipal government
beca	sash worn by students around the neck and reaching down to the feet, it was held in place on one shoulder by a student badge.
blanca	an old copper coin, value half a maravedi
bonete	tippet
cédula	royal order
censo	an annuity
chupa	a sleeveless undercoat
colegios mayores	the premier colleges in the universities Salamanca, Valladolid and Alcalá de Henares
convictor	boarder
cruz	cross
doblón	doubloon
ducado	ducat
ferrado	an old corn measure
legajo	file
limosna	alms, grant
millones	tax introduced in 1590 on four basic foodstuffs, meat, wine, oil and vinegar
parador	state-owned hotel
sempiterna	type of serge
vade, vademecum	a notebook
vara	old measure of about 2.8 feet
veca see *beca*	
vellón	originally applied to coins containing silver, later silver and copper and finally copper only. The word also means wool of one sheep, a fleece.
viaticum	a travel grant
vestuario	clothes, outfit, wardrobe

CHAPTER I

Introduction

The Council of Trent, which ended in 1563, recommended that seminaries should be set up for the teaching and training of aspirants to the priesthood in Catholic countries. This was one of the most important and effective of the measures put forward as part of the Counter-Reformation. However, the foundation of such seminaries in Ireland was impossible from the time of the break with Rome by Henry VIII, the suppression and confiscation of the monasteries and the rigorous laws enforced by him and his successors against those unwilling to renounce the Catholic religion or refusing to subscribe to the Oath of Supremacy. In Ireland the Penal Laws enacted by Henry's successors had disastrous effects on all spheres of Irish life, not least in the area of education, but in particular made it impossible for the establishment, or functioning in the country, of seminaries. The strategy chosen to confront this state of affairs was to establish seminaries *outside* Ireland in Catholic kingdoms sympathetic to the Irish predicament, such as France, Spain,[1] Italy and Portugal and also in Poland, Bohemia and the Low Countries or Spanish Netherlands.[2] So the Irish continental college

---

1 Spain was in the forefront of the Counter-Reformation. At the Council of Trent (three sessions 1545, 1551, 1563) some of the leading theologians were from that kingdom. They included three Dominicans – Fray Domingo de Soto, '*el gran maestro del Concilio*' (the great master of the Council), confessor of the king, of whom it was said in the schools '*qui scit Sotum scit totum*' (he who knows Soto knows all); Fray Francisco de Vitoria from Burgos, professor of theology at the Universities of Valladolid, 1522–6 and Salamanca, 1526–46, defender of the rights of the Indians in S. America; his successor in the chair of theology at Salamanca, Fray Melchor Cano (1509–60). Two eminent Spanish Jesuits, Alfonso Salmerón and Diego Laynez, were also present at the council as the pope's theologians. Ireland was represented by bishops Thomas O'Herlihy (Ross), Eugene O'Hart (Achonry) and Donal McCongail (Raphoe). 2 The terms the 'Netherlands' or 'Low Countries' (in Spanish, *los Paises Bajos*) were for long used to describe the territories of present-day Belgium, Holland, Luxembourg and parts of France which were under the rule of the Habsburgs in the fifteenth century. Before that they were a collection of provinces, duchies and city states. The emperor

movement came into being with the establishment of such foundations for the education of Irish clerical students.[3]

English and Scottish Colleges were also founded on the continent for the same purposes as the Irish establishments. English Colleges for secular clergy were set up at Douai (1568), Rome (1579), Valladolid (1589), Seville (1592), Madrid (1611), Lisbon (1628) and Paris (1667). Scottish Colleges were also set up in Douai (1560), Rome (1600) and Madrid (1627). This last-named college was transferred to Valladolid in 1771.[4]

Two categories of Irish continental colleges emerged from the late sixteenth century – the first, those founded by the major religious orders which had been banished from Ireland, such as the Franciscans, Dominicans,

---

Charles V, who was born and reared in the Netherlands, ruled over seventeen provinces in 1528 – four duchies (Brabant, Gelderland, Limburg and Luxemburg); seven counties (Flanders, Artois, Hainault, Holland, Zeeland, Namur and Zutphen); the margraviate of Antwerp; and five lordships – (Friesland, Mechlin, Utrecht, Overyssel, and Groningen with its dependent districts). The Netherlands were broken up into North and South Netherlands about the year 1579. The Northern part became Protestant as the Dutch Republic or United Provinces. The Southern part, which was under Spanish rule, remained Catholic. This part was known as Spanish Netherlands under Philip II, king of Spain and son of the emperor Charles V. In 1659 Artois (except for St Omer and Aire) came under French rule and some towns in Flanders, Hainault and Luxembourg were ceded to France also. In 1668 France got Lille, Douai, Charleroi, Oundearde, Coutrai and Tournai; some of these were restored to Belgium in 1679 but Valenciennes, Nieuport, St Omer, Ypres and Charlemont were lost. They were partially retaken in 1697. Because some of the towns which changed hands in the various conflicts were places where Irish Colleges were founded, it is necessary to give this brief history at this point. See *Encyclopaedia Britannica*, 13th edition (London, 1926), vols 19–20, p. 416; vols 3–4, pp 673–4. This is an old edition of the encyclopaedia but a good one.   **3** See Rev. T.J.Walsh, *The Irish continental college movement* (Cork, 1973) for an overall picture of the Irish College network, with particular emphasis on the colleges in France.   **4** For information on English and Scottish Colleges see *The first and second diaries of the English College, Douai*, ed. T.F. Knox (London, 1878); A.C.F. Beales, *Education under penalty: English Catholic education from the reformation to the fall of James II, 1547–1689* (London, 1963); M. Murphy, *St Gregory's College, Seville* (CRS, 1992); M.E. Williams, *St Alban's College, Valladolid: four centuries of English Catholic presence in Spain* (London, 1986); Henry Foley, *The annals of the English College, Rome from AD 1579–1773; Records of the English Province of the Society of Jesus* (London, 1883); B.Ward, *Dawn of the Catholic Revival* (London, 1909); Handecoeur, *Histoire du collège anglais Douai* (Reims, 1898).

Augustinians, Capuchins and Carmelites,[5] for the education and training of their own students; the second, those established specifically for the training of secular priests for what was termed, at that time, the 'Irish mission'.[6] In all there were twenty-nine Irish Colleges. Between 1607 and and 1680 twelve were instituted in France, Spain, Portugal, the Low Countries, Italy, Poland and Bohemia by the five religious orders named above. Seventeen colleges for diocesan or secular priests were founded between 1578 and 1689 in France, Spain, Portugal, the Low Countries and Italy. It is worth remembering that, before Ireland figuratively and literally turned her back on Europe in the nineteenth century and faced westward to North America or south-eastward to Australia, our exiles and displaced persons tended to seek refuge in continental Europe, in France, Italy, Spain, Portugal and to a lesser extent further east. Nowadays this fact is largely ignored, forgotten or air-brushed from the collective national memory.

The sixth and seventh centuries have been called the Golden Age of Irish learning, when Ireland was dubbed the 'Island of Saints and Scholars'.[7]

---

5 The Jesuits were in a special category: although banished, they did not set up Irish Colleges on the continent. They were entrusted with the administration of the Irish Colleges for secular priests in Spain and Portugal.　6 Tridentine law required bishops to issue dimissorial letters to clerical students from their dioceses for ordination. Most dioceses in Ireland were, in the seventeenth century, without their bishops who had been forced into exile or, if not exiled, were *in loco refugii*, in hiding. So there were practical difficulties regarding ordination of the students in the Irish Colleges. Pope Paul V in 1614 authorised, in a brief sent to the Irish Colleges in Spain, France, Portugal and the Low Countries, the ordination of students from their colleges *sub titulo missionus*, on the sole title of missionary or pastoral work awaiting them in Ireland. In 1623 Pope Urban VIII extended this privilege to all the Irish Colleges. See T.J.Walsh, op. cit., pp 48–9. This faculty was withdrawn in 1874: see W. McDonald, 'The Irish ecclesiastical colleges since the Reformation – Salamanca', *IER* 10 (1873–4), p. 564. To prevent abuse of the privilege every student had to take an oath that after ordination he would return to Ireland. This subject is treated in some detail in the introduction to Chapter 5. The Jesuits were the administrators of all the Irish Colleges for secular clergy except the Alcalá de Henares college.　7 See J.M. Flood, *Ireland: its saints and scholars* (Dublin, n.d), pp 1–2. 'The sixth and seventh centuries of the Christian era must be regarded as the Golden Age of Ireland. The story of our country during this period is one of the most glorious epochs in the history of European Christianity. Learning became the handmaid of Faith, and art and letters followed rapidly in the train of the churches and monasteries. While Science and Sacred Studies were almost extinguished on the continent owing to the victorious

There were, of course, from the fifth century the great and famous monastic, cathedral, ecclesiastical or lay schools such as Armagh, Bangor, Clonfert, Kildare, Clonard, Clonmacnoise, Lismore, Moville and many others. With the raids of the Danes, the Anglo-Norman invasion of 1160 and the subsequent wars and disturbances throughout the land, the Irish ecclesiastical schools were weakened. By the sixteenth century the great monastic schools had been swept away.[8] There were many other reasons for this including the take-over of clerical positions throughout the parts of the country conquered by the Normans, the isolation of parts of the island still in the hands of petty kings and chieftains coupled with the many internecine wars, and the eventual efforts by the invaders to take over the whole island, not just the areas, such as the Pale, which had become their spheres of influence over centuries.

Universities began to spring up all over the continent from the twelfth century on. Attempts were made to set up one in Ireland in the early fourteenth century but without success.[9] There had been much criticism of the training and education of clerical students in Ireland at that time and especially in the parts still in Gaelic hands. The papal bull *Dum Exquisita*, issued in 1564 by Pope Pius IV, has been described as 'a blueprint for the Irish continental colleges'.[10] Before the Reformation, Irish scholars and clerics had studied at universities throughout Europe. Now in the early seventeenth century the law denied them the right to study at home and forbade them to study at continental seats of learning (and dire consequences followed the breaking of this law).[11]

In the sixteenth century an atmosphere of doubt and disaffection permeated many universities and Reformation influences were prevalent.

advance of the Goths and Vandals, and the civilisation of the East became the prey of Islam, Ireland was the secure abode of European culture. Armagh, Clonard, Durrow, Bangor and Clonmacnoise were at this time the Universities of the West, and the great centres from which the spiritual life was once again to be renewed in Europe'. **8** Edmund Hogan SJ, *Distinguished Irishmen of the sixteenth century* (London, 1894), p. 9. **9** See T.J. Walsh, op. cit., p. 34; Colm Lennon, *Archbishop Richard Creagh of Armagh, 1523–86* (Dublin, 2000), p. 45. **10** T.J. Walsh, op. cit., p. 34. Archbishop Creagh and David Wolfe SJ were nominated by the pope to carry out the ordinances of the bull in Ireland. **11** See Maureen Wall, *The Penal Laws, 1691–1766* (Dublin, 1951); O'Boyle, *The Irish Colleges on the continent* (Dublin, 1835), pp 237–45, in particular the text of the Petition of Fr Richard Berminghan OP to Philip II and the summary of penal enactments, pp 238–42.

Church authorities felt, therefore, that they did not always provide a proper environment for the education of young men as future pastors of the Roman Catholic church. The fathers of Trent, understanding the difficulties and confusions of the time, strongly suggested that Catholic dioceses should have their own colleges to protect the spiritual needs of their students. Bishops were ordered to set up seminaries in their dioceses. The foundation of the Irish Colleges on the European mainland, therefore, put some of the Counter-Reformation policies of the church into force for the Irish church even if at a long remove from its home dioceses.

Out of the total of seventeen Irish Colleges for secular priests, six were located in the Iberian Peninsula, five in Spain (in Salamanca, Santiago de Compostela, Seville, Madrid and Alcalá de Henares) and one in Portugal, in Lisbon. All of the colleges, with the exception of Alcalá de Henares, were run by the Jesuit Order, in spite of the fact that the students being trained were destined to be secular clergy. In Spain the colleges were sited near universities where the collegians generally attended lectures, mainly in arts, philosophy, theology and canon law.[12] Irish students in Portugal had special ties with the universities of Coimbra and Évora since there was no university in Lisbon at that time. The collegians there had to attend classes either in the Jesuit novice house, St Anthony's, or in the Irish Colleges itself. Many of them went on later to study for higher degrees at either of the two Portuguese universities just mentioned.[13]

Trade, war and religion were at the heart of Hiberno-Spanish relations in the early modern period. Spain's Irish dealings had always been a small part of her overall diplomatic strategy. While committed to Catholicism, the Hapsburgs' priorities moved away from the outright support of, say, Philip II. They included hegemony in the Low Countries and the Italian peninsula,[14]

---

12 The foundation dates of the Spanish universities were Salamanca (*c.*1218), Santiago de Compostela (*c.*1504), Seville (*c.*1502), Alcalá de Henares (*c.*1510). There was not a university in Madrid in the sixteenth century. The present Complutense University of Madrid is a transferral of the University of Alcalá which was closed down in the nineteenth century. The University of Alcalá is now in the process of revival.   **13** See Patricia O Connell, *The Irish College at Lisbon, 1590–1834* (Dublin, 2001); 'Irish students at the University of Évora, 1618–1718', *Sea. AM* 20:1 (2004), pp 67–70; *The British Historical Society of Portugal 31st Annual Report and Review*, 2004, pp 59–63. **14** The kingdom of the Two Sicilies was made up of the kingdom of Naples (which was considered the mainland kingdom of Sicily) and the island of Sicily. The Habsburg emperor, Charles V, also king of Spain, ruled the kingdom of Naples as a Spanish dominion and invested his son, Philip II, with the title of king

control of the Spanish Way[15] and dominance on the sea, especially with regard to trade with the American continent, against England and the Dutch rebels. Ireland did ocasionally reach first place during the rule of the Hapsburgs but did not stay there for very long. With the Bourbon succession in 1701 the priorities changed even more dramatically.

The wars, confiscations and plantations of the seventeenth century brought large numbers of Irish exiles to Spain. Because of this, the informal sporadic links between Spain and Catholic Ireland became formal institutions. These included the setting up of a network of Irish Colleges with royal support and the allocation of monies for the payment of the *viaticum* to Irish priests returning to their homeland after ordination,[16] and the widespread employment of Irish soldiers and swordsmen in the royal army,[17] which

of Naples in 1554, with the duchy of Milan in 1546, the Low Countries in 1555, the Spains (Castile, Leon, Aragon and the Indies) in 1556. The kingdom of the Two Sicilies was held by Spain for over two hunred years.   **15** The Spanish Way (*el camino español*) was very important to the Habsburgs. It was a series of overland routes for Spanish troops, through the territories of many rulers, going from Spain and Spanish possessions in Italy, including the duchy of Milan, to the Low Countries. One part of it passed through the Valtellina, a valley leading from Lombardy to the Tyrol and through German states which gave free passage to the Spanish troops. It was a very strategic area contested by many powers and constantly changing hands over the centuries. Spain had problems with her far-flung empire; the sea route through the English Channel was the preferred route for sending troops to the Low Countries, but this route was subject to attack on the sea from Dutch rebels and could only be defended with difficulty at times. It was essential for the Spanish crown to keep the sea and other routes open and well defended at all times. See Geoffrey Parker, *The Army of Flanders and the Spanish Road, 1567–1659* (Cambridge, 2004). **16** The *viaticum* was a grant made by the crown to the newly ordained priest to help him with his travelling expenses for return to Ireland and to provide himself with a suitable disguise so as not to be detected on arrival there. It consisted of 100 ducats. The ducat equalled 11 *reales*, so 100 ducats equalled 1,100 *reales*. Dr Denis O'Doherty, writing in 1914, estimated that 1,200 *reales* were equal to about £12 sterling: *Arch. Hib.*, 3 (1914) p. 92. I have found many and varied opinions of the value of the *real.* **17** The premier Irish regiment in the Spanish service was the regiment of Tyrone, an infantry regiment formed in 1605 and always commanded by the O Neill and often called '*el tercio viejo*', the old brigade. The first of its colonels was Enrique O Neill, son of the Great O Neill; second colonel was his half-brother John; John's illegitimate son, Hugo Enrique, was third colonel; the fourth was Black Hugh, grandson of Art Rua. The fifth colonel was Hugh's brother Art (father of Eoghan Rua). The regiment was disbanded in 1689. Other regiments were *de Ultonia, de Hibernia.* See also Karen Harvey, *The Bellews of Mount Bellew* (Dublin, 1998), pp 98–9.

entailed the setting up of Irish regiments within the Spanish army, and the relief of Irish war widows. After the failed expedition to Kinsale in 1601 Spain, in her desire to suppress the Dutch rebels and make peace with England, changed her approach and, while not completely disengaging from the Irish cause, endeavoured to fulfil her obligations to her defeated Irish allies by the means I have just mentioned. Irish exiles were also given the same rights as Spanish subjects and were eventually and generally integrated into Spanish society, many receiving not only financial support but titles and honours in the process. By the end of the seventeenth century possibilities of military aid had faded somewhat and the *emigrés* became, by necessity, integrated into Spain.[18]

The Irish Colleges depended to a large extent on the generosity of the reigning monarchs of both Spain and Portugal. The Lisbon and Salamanca establishments were endowed by Philip II (1556–98), Santiago de Compostela was supported by Philip III (1598–1621), and Seville, Madrid and Alcalá de Henares were maintained by a mixture of patronage and royal grants. By the eighteenth century most of the colleges were well-established and, if not exactly flourishing, they carried out their functions adequately. They received, educated and fed the collegians who came from all parts of Ireland. However, it would appear that all of the colleges suffered constantly from shortage of funds, due to the acute monetary situation in both Spain and Portugal from time to time, so that grants were frequently in arrears, often for years.[19] It should be pointed out that funding for the college in Santiago de Compostela came generally from the war chest. With the constant wars between Spain and her enemies, this was a chest which was frequently much depleted.

The positive qualities of the colleges were the steady stream of trained clerics who after six or seven years returned to Ireland to carry out the work of the institutional church through an underground priesthood during the sixteenth, seventeenth and eighteenth centuries and even into the nineteenth century. The life of popish priests during the Penal Times in Ireland was, to say the least, difficult and even dangerous. They led a double life to hide their real calling, which must have been an added burden. They lived in

---

18 Micheline Kerney Walsh's collections of documents, *Spanish knights of Irish origin* in four volumes, gives details on distinguished and eminent Irishmen who attained high positions and elevated ranks in the Spanish kingdom. Others, of course, made names for themselves in numerous fields of human endeavour in Spain and her dominions.　　**19** For example, the college was in dire straits from 1686 as the grants had not been paid for 7 years: see Libro de visitas 8 julio 1692, Jesuit Archives – ICOL/SANT/3 (20).

lodgings, watching their step at every turn. By the end of the eighteenth century things began to improve and eventually, even before Catholic Emancipation in the early nineteenth century, the tide began to turn.

The college in Santiago started life in 1605 with twelve students and by 1613 there were ten. Thereafter gaps appear in the available details of numbers. The initial grant from the king, 800 *reales* per year, was to allow the college to support ten students and two priests who in theory at least would be maintained by the amount given. Interestingly, it is specified in an early manuscript that two students from each province Leinster, Munster, Ulster, Connacht and Meath, the old fifth province – were to be received in the college.[20]

While the Irish Colleges in France were immensely important and produced large numbers of secular and order priests for the Irish mission from their several foundations, the colleges in Spain provided a close second. Irish links with Spain were of long standing. They were first and foremost religious because of a common faith and, in the aftermath of the Protestant Reformation, had attained a new solidarity. Commercial and fishing interests also provided links. Dublin, Waterford, Galway and Limerick traded with Bilbao, La Coruña and Cádiz, exchanging fish, hides and timber for iron, salt and wine. Irish trade with the other kingdom in the peninsula was important also, as Lisbon was the great bustling centre of transatlantic commerce and the exotic and lucrative Asian and African trade.[21]

Notwithstanding the multiplicity of significant events in eighteenth-century Spain and Portugal, I think that it would be fair to say that two stand out as directly affecting the Irish Colleges in both these kingdoms – firstly, the disastrous earthquake of 1755 in Lisbon, when the Irish College there was extensively damaged, and, secondly, the suppression and confiscation of the property of the Jesuit Order, which occurred in Portugal in 1759 and in Spain in 1767.[22]

By the end of the eighteenth century many of the colleges were going into decline. There were, of course, at least three events in Ireland which had profound consequences also for the decline and closure of the Irish continental colleges. The first of these was the evident failure of the Penal Laws which finally became obvious to the authorities in Ireland as well as

---

20 Sal. Arch. S 34/2, f. 3, the document is dated April 1613. **21** See P. O Connell, *The Irish College at Lisbon, 1590–1834*, p. 115. **22** The Jesuits were suppressed in France in 1764, and 1773 by the pope, Clement XIV (1767–74). Reinstatement came in 1814.

the realisation that many of these laws could no longer be enforced. The edict of registration of 'popish clergy' in 1703 was in itself an admission of the failure of almost two centuries of cruel and unjust laws.[23] A consequence of the easing of many of the more severe penal laws was that bishops were retaking their dioceses. Because of the severe shortage of diocesan priests they were forced to ordain large numbers to the priesthood.[24] This in itself was the cause of many problems.[25] The other two events in Ireland were, of course, the setting up of St Patrick's College, or seminary, in 1795 in Maynooth, Co. Kildare, with the blessing of the British government, and the long-awaited passing of the Catholic Emancipation Bill in 1829.

The decision of the government to set up the Maynooth college may have been prompted by fear of the ideas of the French Revolution penetrating into an Ireland teetering on the brink of rebellion, which came to a head in 1798, as well as an acknowledgment that the penal code and prohibition of 'popish priests' had not been exactly successful. There were also constant fears of a French invasion.[26] There certainly was concern that the priests returning to Ireland had not alone been continental-trained but that the majority had received that training in the several Irish Colleges in *ancien régime* France and might conceivably be contaminated with ideas of liberty, fraternity and equality.[27]

As I said already, the closure of the Irish Colleges was not entirely due to Irish circumstances; some closures were due to political circumstance in Spain itself. Some of the colleges were subsumed into Salamanca when the Jesuits were suppressed. So, a combination of events both in Ireland and in Spain militated against the continuance of the old Irish Colleges which had served Ireland well for hundreds of years. As the situation improved in Ireland in the nineteenth century, local seminaries began to appear, and by the mid-century were turning out well-educated young men as priests.

23 See Act for Registration of Popish Clergy 1703, with *Register of 1704* (Dublin, 1703).   **24** The shortage was due firstly to the closing of many of the colleges when the Jesuits were suppressed in France, Spain and Portugal and eventually to the closures of those remaining in Revolutionary times.   **25** They had to be ordained without training and were required to go to a continental college after ordination so that ill-equipped and uneducated clerics were often found. This was a throw-back to the pre-Trent situation in Ireland.   **26** At times this fear reached paranoic proportions, as witnessed by the widespread building of Martello towers as coastal lookouts throughout Ireland and England at that time.   **27** O'Boyle states that the Irish College Paris had a third of the Irish students who were studying on the continent for the secular priesthood, op. cit., p. 54.

Catholic education benefitted from the easing of restrictions and finally rendered the continental colleges superfluous.

Before the foundation of Maynooth there had been much talk of mitigation of the disabilities on Catholics. Fr Michael Daly, who was rector of the Irish College at Lisbon from 1778 to 1799, had a longstanding exchange of letters with the Dominican archbishop of Dublin, Dr John Thomas Troy (1786–1823).[28] Fr Daly had received a copy of the archbishop's pastoral letter and in his letter of thanks, dated 27 August 1795, mentions the proposed legislation by the British government regarding what he called 'not total emancipation but some liberty being granted for the propagation of learning amongst our people'. He says 'the restriction laid on it by Law is the most barbarous and inhuman of all their penal laws'. In his following letter he pursues the subject and affirms:

> Our emancipation, as it is termed, is not far distant, and it would seem, the fever of our slavery is coming to a crisis. What I long for is the Act of Parliament itself for the projected establishment for Catholic Education. I hope it is done with a liberality of Sentiment and fund that will render it really useful, and such as will answer all our wants in that line. If this is the case, we may shut up our doors on this side of the Water; as I suppose no one will seek abroad with inconvenience, what he can conveniently find at home.[29]

Although it was some years before the closure of the last three colleges, these were prophetic words. Lisbon closed in 1834 (and was subsequently sold to a religious order), Alcalá in 1884 and Salamanca, the last outpost, in the period 1951–7. Lisbon had been taken over by the Portuguese state in 1910; both Alcalá and Salamanca could have been retained by the Irish state, but economic considerations let them slip away. The Irish college in Paris was retained and it is now a prestigious Irish cultural centre, having been extensively, and beautifully, refurbished before it reopened officially in 2003 as the Centre Culturel Irlandais. An Irish presence in Salamanca and Alcalá would have been of great benefit for generations of students from all parts of Ireland in this twenty-first century.

---

28 Before translation to Dublin he was bishop of Ossory from 1776 to 1786.
29 Dublin Diocesan Archives, letter from Fr Michael Daly to Archbishop Troy of Dublin dated 18 April 1795.

INTRODUCTION

List of the Irish Colleges or seminaries founded on the continent

Date	Town	Kingdom	Founder	Status	Other details
1578	Paris	France	Fr John Lee of Dublin or Meath	secular	closed, 1793; reopened 1804, now Centre Culturel Irlandais
1590	Lisbon	Portugal	Fr John Howling SJ from Wexford	secular	closed, confiscated in 1759; re-opened, 1782; finally closed, 1834
1592	Salamanca	Spain	Fr Thomas White SJ from Clonmel, Co.Tipperary	secular	closed, 1951–7
1594	Douai	Low Countries[30] (France)	Fr Christopher Cusack SJ from Co. Meath	secular	confiscated, 1793[31]
1600	Antwerp	Low Countries (Belgium)	Fr Christopher Cusack SJ and his cousin Laurence Sedgrave	secular	closed, 1793
1603	Bordeaux	France	Fr Dermot McCarthy[32] Muskerry, Co. Cork & Cardinal Archbishop de Sourdis of Bordeaux	secular	closed, 1796
1605	Santiago de Compostela	Spain	Fr Thomas White SJ	secular	closed, 1767[33]

30 See footnote 2.   31 Most of the Irish Colleges in France were confiscated or suppressed during the Revolutionary government of France. See O'Boyle, op. cit., p. 235.   32 Fr McCarthy was son of Sir Callaghan Mac Teige Mac Carthy, fifteenth Lord of Muskerry, by his first wife, Ellen, daughter of James, Lord Barry: cf. T.J.Walsh, op. cit., p. 87. Fr Walsh points out that, according to the MacCarthy Muskerry pedigree as found in the Carew MSS, v. 635, f. 154 r (Lambeth Library), Diarmuid Mac Carthy, priest, is noted as the son of Callaghan MacTeige. 33 Suppression of the Jesuits in Spain.

[25]

(continued)		**Irish Colleges or seminaries founded on the continent**			
Date	Town	Kingdom	Founder	Status	Other details
1607	Louvain	Low Countries	Archbishop Florence Conry OFM	Franciscan	St Anthony's
1610	Lille	do.	Archdukes[34] and Fr Francis Nugent	secular	suppressed, 1793
1612	Rouen	France	Fr Gelasius Lurcan	secular	little known about this college
1612	Seville	Spain	Theobald Stapleton from Cashel, Co. Tipperary	secular	closed; 1767 subsumed into Salamanca
1616	Tournai	Low Countries Belgium	Fr Christopher Cusack SJ	secular	little known about this college
1620	Charleville	France	Fr Francis Nugent OFM Cap	Capuchin	transferred to Bar-sur-Aube & Vassy in Champagne
1620	Prague	Bohemia[35]		Franciscan	
1623	Louvain	Low Countries Belgium	Archbishop Eugene McMahon or Mathews	secular	closed, 1797; *Collegium Pastorale*
1625	Rome	Italy	Luke Wadding OFM	Franciscan	St Isidore's still in existence
1628	Rome	Italy	Luke Wadding and Cardinal Ludovisi	secular	still in existence
1626	Louvain	Low Countries	Richard Bermingham OP & Archdukes	Dominican	

34 The Archdukes, the joint rulers of Spanish Netherlands, were Albert, son of the Emperor Maximilian II, and his wife, the Infanta Clara Eugenia, daughter of Philip II and Elizabeth of Valois. **35** The kingdom of Bohemia was also ruled by the Habsburgs from 1562 to 1918.

(continued)			**Irish Colleges or seminaries founded on the continent**		
Date	Town	Kingdom	Founder	Status	Other details
1629	Madrid	Spain	Theobald Stapleton, Cashel, Co. Tipperary	secular	absorbed into Salamanca
1645	Vielun	Poland		Franciscan	
1649	Alcalá de Henares	Spain	Baron Jorge Silveira Paz	secular	closed, 1785; subsumed into Salamanca
1656	Rome	Italy		Augustinian	S. Matteo Merulana
1656	Capranica	Italy		Franciscan	
1659	Lisbon	Portugal	Dominic O Daly OP	Dominican	Corpo Santo church still exists: Irish Dominican parish in Cascais.
1660	Toulouse	France	Anne of Austria		closed, 1783.
1665	La Rochelle	France		Carmelite	
1677	Rome	Italy		Dominican	S. Clemente: still in operation
1677	Aix-la-Chapelle	France		Carmelite[36]	
1689	Nantes	France	Archbishop of Nantes	secular	suppressed, 1793

A Jesuit foundation was established at Poitiers in 1674. Not a seminary, this was a lay school for the education of Catholic youth. It was set up by Catherine of Braganza, wife of Charles II of England. It was suppressed in 1762.[37]

36 T.J.Walsh, op. cit., p. 4.   **37** Ibid., p. 84, writes that it had two burses, given by Mrs John O'Meagher, Co. Tipperary, with capital value of 16,000 francs and three with a value of 30,000 livres invested in East India bonds by Mr Jeremiah O'Crowley, Cork. They were transferred to the Irish College at Paris at the closure of the college in Poitiers.

CHAPTER 2

Santiago de Compostela

Given the centuries-old connections between the Celtic realms of Galicia and Ireland, it is not without significance that the dawn of the seventeenth century, when Gaelic civilisation was about to collapse, Galicia and especially Santiago de Compostela would provide sanctuary, shelter and support for numerous Irish refugees and a centre for the preservation and promotion of education and culture for their compatriots – the Irish College at Santiago.

The early places of Christian pilgrimage were Jesusalem, Rome[1] and Santiago de Compostela. Santiago de Compostela did not rank as high as the holy places associated with the life of Jesus or with Rome and its special links with the Apostles. Other places of pilgrimage, such as Puy in France, Canterbury, Walsingham, Holywell and St Andrew's in Britain, Portiuncula (Assisi) and Loretto in Italy, sprang up later. Indeed, our own places of pilgrimage dedicated to the national apostle are respectably ancient also. St Patrick's purgatory in Lough Derg island was well-known in Europe in mediaeval times as attested by its appearance in Hungarian, Spanish and other manuscripts. Co. Mayo's Holy Mountain, Croagh Patrick, was revered even in pre-Christian times.[2]

---

[1] Rome, where St Peter had moved the centre of the Church from Antioch in AD 42. By 313, before the fall of Rome, Constantine had declared Christianity the official religion of the Roman Empire. [2] For an interesting slant on St James and Ireland and the myth of his supposed Irish visit see Dr María del Henar Velasco López (University of Salamanca), 'Divus Iacobus in Ibernia' in *Lógos Hellenikos, Homenaje al Profesor Gaspar Morocho Gayo, Universidad de León* (2003). Dr Velasco López, a philologist, spent some time in the Dublin Institute for Advanced Studies where, she says, her interest was fired by Dr S. Ua Súilleabháin in the Irish who came to Spain in the seventeenth century and especially the works of Philip O'Sullivan, the eminent scholar and historian, cousin of Donal O'Sullivan Beare and author of *Historiae Catholicae Iberniae compendium and Patritiana Decas*. See also Ofelia Rey Castelao, 'Exiliados irlandeses en Santiago de Compostela desde fines del XVI a mediados del XVII' in Enrique García Hernán, Miguel Ángel Bunes, Oscar Recio Morales (eds), *Irlanda y la*

Tradition has it that St James the Apostle came to Spain to evangelise and to carry out his mission. Later he returned to Jerusalem, was captured and martyred by decapitation there, probably in Caesarea, by Herod Agrippa in *c*.44 AD. Some of his Spanish disciples rescued his body after burial in Palestine and sailed from Jaffa back to Spain with it. They landed in Padrón, then the Roman port of Iria Flavia, called after the Emperor Flavius Vespasius. The saint's body was buried in a Roman cemetery there. With the religious persecution of the Christians by the Romans, the location was lost and forgotten and was only re-discovered eight hundred years later in 813. Another version is that in the tenth century the relics of the saint were transferred miraculously from Jerusalem to Compostela where they were found and where the present cathedral and shrine were erected.

The story of the rediscovery of the sepulchre is that a hermit, Pelayo, saw a bright star hang over a certain field and heard sacred music emanating from a wood nearby. The bishop of the diocese of Iria Flavia, Teodomiro, had the field dug up when this was reported to him. A small stone construction was found which contained the bodies of the saint and his two disciples, Atemasio and Teodomiro. A small oratory was built near the spot by Alfonso II, the Chaste (789–842) and in the course of time a Benedictine monastery was founded there to guard the sepulchre. From this early foundation the city of Santiago de Compostela grew and became a shrine, and the name Santiago de Compostela, St James of the field of the star, came to mean one of the great places of devotion in Christiandom.[3] St James became the patron saint of Spain and was associated with the overthrow, after many centuries, of the occupying Moors. The name, *Matamoros* (one who kills Moors), now considered objectional, was often applied to the saint (who obviously was not involved in such activities).

Irish pilgrims are known to have made the journey to the shrine of St James[4] down through the centuries. Those who travelled there would have

monarquía hispánica Kinsale 1601–2001: guerra, política, exilio y relegación (Madrid, 2002), pp 89–111.   **3** In Latin the name is *campus stellae* (field of the star). Many theories have been put forward to explain the name. The city was called in English St Iago of Compostella, in French St Jacques and in Spanish San Iago or San Jacomé Apóstol.   **4** An old hospital at St Lazar's Hill, Townsend Street, Dublin was founded for pilgrims or crusaders setting out for, or returning from, places of pilgrimage such as the Holy Land or Santiago. St Lazarus is sometimes equated with Lazarus, a leper, cured in the gospel of St Luke, 16:20 and may have been based also on Lazarus, the brother of saints Martha and Mary Magdalene who was raised from the dead by Jesus. St Lazarus is the patron saint of lepers. The

had their tombs decorated with the symbol of their journey, a scallop shell or *concha* which has traditionally been carried proudly by pilgrims to the city. It still is, as well as the *bordón*, or staff, which is referred to as *la tercera pierna del caminante* (the third leg of the traveller), the *escarcala*, the pouch, the *calabaza*, the gourd, and the *patenôtre*, the chaplet or hood.

The sons of Zebedee and Maria Salome, James and John, were two of the earliest of Christ's disciples. After the Cruxifixion when the disciples scattered over the world – Mathew to Ethiopia, Jude to Persia, Simon and Thomas to India, Bartholomew to Armenia and so on – it was as though Jesus allocated the world to his disciples and gave the Roman province of Spain to St James or James Boanerges: 'Dum Paterfamilia/Rex Universorum/ Donaret provincias/Jus Apostolorum.'[5]

Santiago de Compostela is located between the rivers Tambre and Ulla which flow into the *rías* of Muros y Noya and Arosa. *Rías* are the typical fiord-like inlets of the area of the west coast of Galicia in the region named Las Rías Bajas. Padrón, ten miles up-stream, is the main port of the Ria de Arosa and was also the port where St James landed when he came to preach the gospel in Galicia.[6] Padrón later became an episcopal see

fifteenth century appears to have been the time of most early Irish pilgrims. See the *Annals of the Four Masters* (ed. John O'Donovan, 1856), and *Annala Uladh*, ed. Stalley and Halliday et al. Some early Irish pilgrims were Finghin Mór O Driscoll and his son, Tadhg, who sailed from Dunasead Castle, Baltimore, Co. Cork to pray at Santiago (T.J. Walsh, op. cit., p. 56). There were many pilgrims from past centuries, including Chaucer's famous Wife of Bath in the *Canterbury Tales* who had been 'to Galice at Saint Jame'. The many modern visitors included Walter Starkie, a former professor of Spanish at TCD, Dublin and author of *Spanish raggle taggle*. The Holy Year (*Año Santo Compostelano*) or Jubilee Year is celebrated every few years in Santiago de Compostela since the twelfth century. The Hospital Real, the Royal Hospice for pilgrims in the magnificent Plaza del Obradoiro, Santiago, was set up by the Reyes Católicos. It has been restored in recent years and is now a luxurious five-star hotel, El parador de los reyes. See also *The pilgrim's guide to Santiago de Compostela* (*c.*1140), criticial edition and annotated translation by Paula Gerson et al. (London, 1997). **5** The name given to the two brothers by Jesus for their great enthusiasm for his teachings, means 'Sons of Thunder'. See José Miguel Ruiz Morales, *The Tablet* (London), 30 January 1954 and *Estrellas, conchas y espadas*, Ministerio de Asuntos Exteriores – Escuela Diplomática (Madrid, 1953). Dr Declan Downey has pointed out to me that this hymn is included in The Chieftains' marvellous CD, *Santiago*. It is one of the medieval songs sung by the pilgrims on the *camino* since time immemorial. **6** The stone to which the boat was tied is preserved with great reverence in Padrón.

which was eventually moved to Santiago de Compostela when it became the spiritual capital of Galicia and St James the patron saint of all Spain. *Santiago y cierra España* (St James and close Spain) became the battle-cry in the fight to rid Spain of the Moors. Santiago has a dominant position in Spanish tradition even to the extent of taking over the name of a starry group, the Milky Way, *Via Lactea*, which is popularly called 'El camino de Santiago' (The route of St James). This arises from the tradition that in the Middle Ages the pilgrims from every country in Europe crossed the Pyrenees at Roncesvalles[7] and, guided by the the Milky Way, made their journey on foot all through the north of Spain, over the 500-mile-long *camino* to Santiago de Compostela. His feast day is celebrated on 25 July.

Galicia, bounded by the Atlantic on its north-west coast, must have seemed like an ideal place for the Irish Catholics fleeing Ireland from the oppressive laws of an alien government at the end of the sixteenth and beginning of the seventeenth centuries. A long tradition of commerce along the trade routes to the north of Spain,[8] a common Celtic background, the fishing by Spanish fleets around the Irish coast for centuries together with the fact that Spain was the champion of the Catholic Church at the time of the Reformation, and, indeed, possibly the religious significance of the city of Santiago which had drawn Irish there for centuries – all these factors combined to make the Iberian peninsula the goal of the exiled Irish.

However, when the first wave of Irish arrived, mainly at the port of La Coruña, things were far from ideal for an influx of destitute foreigners, many of them aristocratic figures and their followers, fleeing from possible capture and imprisonment in the Tower of London from which few escaped execution as traitors. This was during the years following the failed Desmond revolt in Munster, and later after the defeat at Kinsale and was not, however, an opportune moment to descend on the kingdom of Galicia.

Dr Ofelia Rey Castelao of the University of Santiago, who has written extensively on the subject of Irish exiles in Galicia, points out[9] that many of them found their way to Santiago de Compostela at a moment when the kingdom was going through hard times.[10] She cites three phases of

---

7 A village in the Pyrenees famous for the defeat of Charlemagne and the death of Roland, cf. *Le Chanson de Roland*.   **8** The main ports in the north of Spain used by the Irish were La Coruña (called in English La Groyne or Corunna; the form in *gallego* is A Coruña), Bayona and Bilbao. Nowadays place names are given in *gallego* in Galicia. A lot of this trade was clandestine and certainly the conveying of seminarians to Spain was illegal.   **9** See footnote 2, op. cit., pp 89–111.   **10** Dr Castelao quotes,

Irish immigration (1) 1570–83; (2) death of Philip II in 1598 until 1607 (the flight of the Earls); and (3) from the flight to the aftermath of the 1641 rebellion up to 1653. Our main concern is with the period 1604 to 1607 and thereafter, and includes the most important of all the immigrants into Galicia – Domhnall Cam Ó Súillebháin Beara (Donal O'Sullivan Beare), who arrived in Galicia in 1604.

The influx of the Irish to this holy place must have caused many headaches for the authorities. Those who had their churches, monasteries or convents taken over or levelled in Ireland could be accommodated in the many monasteries or convents in the area; soldiers could be absorbed into regiments in the Spanish service; however, the lay people were in a different situation. After Kinsale many of those arriving were nobles whose lands had been confiscated and who had to leave in a hurry with little baggage. Domhnall Cam Ó Súilleabháin Beara, Prince of Beara, was the principal of these after Kinsale. He came with a large retinue of followers as well as several priests who had been chaplains to the the fighting men.[11]

The finance for the maintenance of several hundred family members and private armies was a burden, logically, for the king but was often put on the taxes of the kingdom of Galicia, a poor region with tax sourced mainly from the peasants. The governor, the Conde de Caracena, was sympathetic to the exiles but of necessity had to make frequent requests to the king for subsidies on their behalf. In the case of O'Sullivan Beare the details of payments give us an idea of the extent of the problem.[12]

The Irish College in Santiago was set up in 1605 but was already planned in previous years by Philip II, champion of the Catholic Church, who had already made a grant to the Irish students even before the college was

op. cit., p. 90, from a *Memorias del Arzobispado de Santiago*, the original of which was published in or around 1607. It paints a picture of the town at that time as 'dirty, dark, with narrow, ugly streets, badly paved with some houses and towers which are well built but generally very old and also ugly, somewhat narrow and dark because they are overcrowded and without courtyards'. This is certainly not a picture of Santiago at the present time.   **11** See Micheline Kerney Walsh, *Arch. Hib.* 45, 'O'Sullivan Beare in Spain: some unpublisted documents', 1990, pp 51–5; she lists eleven gentlemen, some with their families in Spain, others who had to leave them behind and who are in great want, six priests and twelve of his followers who accompanied O'Sullivan and were then residing in Valladolid. While Madrid was the capital from 1561, the court was moved to Valladolid from 1601 to 1606. Hereafter O'Sullivan Beare is generally referred to under the English form of his name, Donal O'Sullivan or Donal Cam.   **12** M. Walsh, ibid., pp 54–5.

instituted. He died in 1598 before he could put his plan into action. The emphasis in this work is on information about life in the college from the points of view of finances, courses and so on, the identity of the rectors, the students, the main events and collegians, and others connected with the college, who distinguished themselves in various ways. Sources are scarce, fragmented, often non-existent. However, a picture does emerge of a college based on sound principles and which over its life span successfully carried out the objects for which it was founded – to train priests fit to return to Ireland and succour the people and help them in every way possible in their spiritual life.

The Jesuits themselves had only recently established a college in Santiago de Compostela. According to Ofelia Rey Castelao, they had been frustrated in their attempts to control the university in the middle of the sixteenth century and they were not, in fact, able to set up their own college until the time of Archbishop D. Francisco Blanco, who had already promoted the Jesuits in his earlier areas of control, Ourense and Malaga. He also gave them a building and the income needed to maintain it (the Royal College). She also states that prior to the founding of the Irish College several Irish received education in that college and she is of the opinion that from it grew the germ of St Patrick's which the Irish College was eventually called.[13]

In the early years of the foundation of the college in Santiago de Compostela the Irish found it difficult to secure a suitable house. Couselo[14] tells us that they were housed badly in a variety of rented dwellings. The earliest of these was in the Huertas quarter of the city. In 1613 Molina Canty[15] complained in a memorial to Philip III that he and the rest of the

13 Ofelia Castelao, op. cit., p 92. According to E. Rivera Vázquez, *Galicia y los jesuitas* (Santiago, 1989), p. 421 (hereafter referred to as Rivera). The Irish College was the only international centre which existed in Santiago at that time.   14 José Couselo Bouzas, *El colegio de irlandeses de Santiago de Compostela* (Santiago, 1935), p. 9 (hereafter referred to as Couselo). Fr Conway, the first Jesuit rector, in what appears to be a draft of a petition regarding the acquisition of a suitable house, refers to the ten days he is in Santiago trying desperately to get a house '*y sacar estos estudiantes del Arenal donde estan que es el lugar mas infame de toda la ciudad*' (and get the students out of *el Arenal* (literally the sandpit) where they are which is the most infamous place in all the city). By which I take it that they were in an area of ill-repute. Sal. Arch. 33/1/15.   15 This man is mentioned by Fr Patrick Sinnott (for further information of Sinnott see chapters 5 and 6). He was a bachelor of Arts and had been a student in the college prior to 1613 when it was not specifically a seminary. He left for Ireland and later married. The name is

Irish students who were studying in this city by order of His Majesty suffered great poverty and lack of appropriate lodging. He added that a lot of money was spent on rented accommodation and the finance which the king gave them was too little for their needs. He pointed out that the king had some grace-and-favour houses in the Rua del Camino and Algalia de Abaxo which His Majesty might grant them with the object of making their economic situation less precarious.

On instruction, the mayor of Santiago sought information on the matter. He was told by one witness that the house in the Huertas district was 'neither comfortable nor sufficient' (*no es comoda ni suficiente*). Although a royal order of concession of the houses was given no action took place because of litigation and other problems.[16]

In 1616 the rector of the Irish College, Richard Conway SJ, rented a house in Rua Nova (Nueva) for the college and bought it in 1620 from the university for 1,020 ducats.[17] This was no. 44 Rua Nova and it became the permanent home of Irish students fleeing from religious intolerance and persecution in the Ireland of penal times. The garden at the back of the house includes a statue of the patron saint of Ireland to whom the college was dedicated. At the top of the facade of the building which is sandwiched between houses of the same height there is the royal *escudo* or coat of arms, surmounted by a crown which indicated royal protections for the college and its students. On the opposite side of the narrow arched street is the parish church, no. 27, of Santa María Salomé, mother of the SS. James and John, wife of Zebedee.[18]

In 1770 after the expulsion of the Jesuits, the college was taken over and the state occupied it. Couselo gives us a description of the college taken from the document produced by the officer designated by His Majesty to sequester the building.[19] It describes the structure in minute detail and refers to the back exit on to Rua Villar. In the back garden there was a well with a stone basin, around the garden was a vine arbour, on the east side of the garden there was a privy connected to the first floor; on the north

given variously as Molina Kanty and Canty Molina, see Couselo, op. cit., p. 9.
16 Couselo, op. cit., p. 10.   **17** Rivera, op. cit., p. 433.   **18** This ancient church is still the parish church and on a recent visit to the city I attended Sunday mass there which was the occasion of the first holy communion of the children of the parish. An interesting feature of this church is the statue at the entrance of *La virgen embarazada* (The pregnant virgin).   **19** Couselo, op. cit., pp 29–33.

side there was an exit with a stable which could be used as a pigsty; off the entrance hall there was the chapel and the refectory with a wooden floor and a kitchen with a fireplace, sink and door to the garden; there were other rooms including larders, a cellar and a wood store. On the first floor in the front was the rector's room and study, a bedroom and library and another salon. The dormitories were on other floors.

The statue of St Patrick which occupied a niche in a wall in the garden was a special and revered representation of the national saint of Ireland. Couselo suggests that the sculpture was probably the work of Mateo de Prado who also composed the choir of St Martin's, a noted seventeenth-century sculptor. Several Irish ex-patriate merchants were mentioned in the college ledger in 1667 as subscribing 300 *reales* to the purchase of the figure.[20]

The Irish College in Santiago was often referred to as *el seminario irlandés* by the Jesuits of the Royal College in Santiago, the principal Jesuit institution in the city, to which the Irish College was subject. This was to distinguish it from their own college. In the *Catalogii* of the Society in Spain the distinction is made very clear: the *Colegio de Santiago* is the Royal College, the *Seminario irlandés* is the Irish College. However, this may not be merely a simple distinction.[21] The college is variously referred to as *el colegio irlandés de Santiago, el colegio de S. Patricio, el colegio de nobles irlandeses, el colegio de niños irlandeses* or *el seminario*. I have already mentioned the two categories of Irish Colleges on the continent – those set up by the regular clergy (the Dominicans, Franciscans and others, to educate their own clerical students) and those dedicated to the training of the aspirants to the secular priesthood. However, in Spain the descriptive element attached to *colegio* is important and is more specialised and complex than in English. Questions relating to it have been debated over centuries. Perhaps the use of the word 'seminary' classified the Irish Colleges as somewhat outside the ambit of the *colegio* proper.[22]

---

20 Ibid., op. cit., p. 21; Sal. Arch. 34/2, f. 72.   **21** See Catálogos públicos de la Provincia de Castilla, 1597–1660, Cat. MSS. Hib. SJ – Jesuit Archive, Dublin. **22** Under the heading, *Tipología colegial,* the authors of a scholarly work on the history of the *colegio convento* in Mexico have teased out the subject and documented and analysed the multiple expressions denoting colleges in Spain, *colegio secular, colegio universitario, colegio regular, colegio real, colegio convento* and the wider distinction of *colegio mayor and colegio menor.* See Manuel Casado Arboniés and Francisco Casado Arboniés, *Historia y proyección en la Nueva España de una institución educativa: el colegio-convento de carmelitas descalzos de la*

The Jesuits governed the Irish College in Santiago de Compostela by royal order from 1613 until the suppression of the Order in Spain in 1767. It would be reasonable to suppose that the course of study in the college would have been heavily influenced by the Jesuit theories of education, interlaced with the general norms of education for clerical students throughout Spain at that time. The *ratio studiorum*, the Jesuit system of education, was very highly esteemed in Catholic countries in the wake of the vigorous Counter-Reformation and was also highly regarded even in Protestant countries.

We have, however, little specific or documented evidence or information about the course of study in the college. After some years of Jesuit administration in the two Irish College of Salamanca and Santiago de Compostela a rationalisation was reached; it was decided at some time around 1626 that the seminarians should spend two or three years in Santiago in pursuit of an arts and philosophy course (*artistas*) and then having got satisfactory results in examination they should proceed to the Irish College in Salamanca. There they would spend a further three years in the study of theology before final ordination. This was changed for a while in 1748. Denis O'Doherty[23] tells us that the procedure was dropped for a time during the rectorship of John O'Brien (1743–60) in Salamanca because of friction between the rectors of the two Irish Colleges. O'Brien succeeeded in getting students direct from Ireland to study arts as well as theology in Salamanca.

The collegians in Santiago attended classes at the university for the arts course which was a *trienio*, a three-year course in arts and philosophy. As we know at that time these courses included many subjects, such as logic, rhetoric, natural science, political science, poetics, philosophy of nature, physics, metaphysica and the four liberal arts: arithmetic, geometry, perspective and music. Before 1613 the Irish students attended classes mainly in *gramática*, for which a competence in Latin was required. After the Jesuit takeover classes in arts and philosophy were held in the Jesuit college and were often given by Irish Jesuits. Some of the students did become licenciates of the university before going on to Salamanca for their theological studies. The students undoubtedly read *súmulas*, compendiums

Universidad Alcalá de Henares (1570–1835) (Alcalá, 2001), pp 41–55. Rivera, op. cit., p. 421, refers to the Irish College as *colegio seminario*. **23** *Arch. Hib.* 4 (1915), 'Students of the Irish College, Salamanca', p. 33, fn.2.

of logic, which were used in Alcalá de Henares university and in most colleges at the time.[24]

The student's day in Santiago, we are told by Rivera, would have followed that of a novice in the Jesuit order. Early rising was at 5.30 in winter and 4.30 in summer; mental prayer followed until mass at 6.30, then private study in his room by the student until leaving for classes. The seminarians went there in twos. On their return, the litany of the Virgin was recited before their main meal during which there was a reading from a spiritual work. This was followed by a period of rest overseen by the superior or another father. Then there was a brief exposition on a moral theme or on the lives of the saints.

Later the students recited the rosary and read a spiritual work in private. Classes came then or else private study, often followed by a Scholastic debate. Before supper the litanies of the saints, were said, there was a short period of recreation, and a quarter of an hour for examination of conscience before retiring to bed.[25]

Preaching and debating were emphasised at that time; the Jesuits were very adept in both these fields and are credited with 'the revival of religious zeal in the latter part of the sixteenth century' in Spain.[26] In the Irish College, Salamanca, the students often attended at the Royal College for *Dominicales*, a debate which took the form of a dialectic between two students who had to argue from opposing sides in a discussion. They studied moral and dogmatic theology. The theological courses in Salamanca would have been strongly influenced by the teachings of Robert Bellarmine SJ and the many other renowned Spanish theologians of the time – Suárez, de Soto, Molina and others already mentioned.

After their three-year course in theology and their ordination, the seminarians were supposed to go back immediately to Ireland. The majority did, in fact, return, but a few became Jesuits and only a small proportion of these went back to their native land. They were often sent to missionary countries. There are indeed, several instances of requests from the Jesuit Provincial in Ireland for the repatriation of individuals for

24 See Patricia O Connell, 'Francisco de Quevedo's study of philosophy in the University of Alcalá de Henares', *BHS*, 5:3 (July 1972), pp 256–64 for details of the full course read at that university before 1600.   **25** Rivera, op. cit., p. 432. **26** R. Trevor Davies, *The Golden Century of Spain, 1501–1621* (London, 1937), p. 288, who also tells us that in Spain 'Preaching was regarded as the prerogative of monks; so much so that parish priests and other seculars were liable to give offence if they attempted it.'

the Irish mission. These were not always acceded to. If a student joined the
Jesuits or another religious order, he was automatically absolved from his
oath promising to return to Ireland. As Jesuits, the students were subject
to the jurisdiction of the Provincial or the General of the Order in Rome.
In fact, many of them were sent all over the Spanish spheres of influence
or were retained in that kingdom for teaching or missionary purposes.

The archbishop of Santiago, don Bartolomé Rajoy, in the course of a
letter, dated 1767, to the Conde de Aranda, first minister of the kingdom
of Spain explained his appointment of a local parish priest as acting-
superior of the Irish College, at the time of the suppression of the Society
of Jesus in that year by the government of Aranda. His explanation was,
firstly, that the parish priest lived opposite the college, that he was the
parish priest of the church of Sta. María Salomé and that it was convenient
to appoint him to oversee the direction of the college at a crucial time and,
secondly, that the education of the seminarians was taken care of by others
qualified to do so. In the process he refers to the attendance of the students
at the principal Jesuit college in the city, the Royal College, for the three arts
courses, for the three years, where they received lessons from Dr Blanco, a
Scotist and fellow of Fonseca College.[27] He also points out that afterwards
they went on to Salamanca to study theology and other subjects required
by the ministry to which they were dedicated.

27 Couselo, op. cit., p. 17. The archbishop refers to a three year course in the
Royal College which according to other sources had for long been reduced to two
years. Fonseca college in the university of Salamanca was founded by Archbishop
Alonso de Fonseca, who was appointed archbishop of Santiago de Compostela in
1507. This college is sometimes called the *colegio del arzobispo* and became the Irish
College, Salamanca from 1827 to 1830, and from 1857 until the 1950s.

CHAPTER 3

College Life

In order to understand the complexities of the financial situation of the Irish College it is necessary to address the question of currency and coinage in Spain in the seventeenth and eighteenth centuries. Before the standardisation of coinage in most European countries in the nineteenth century, the operation of a currency system must have been nothing short of a nightmare. In Spain, the diversity and complexity of the coinage was no exception and the system of weights and measures was no less so.

In this work the accounting system from 1613 onwards needs some elucidation. At the time of the Jesuits taking over the running of the Irish College the main coinage in circulation was the *ducado*, a gold coin, used in Castile from 1497, the *real*, a silver coin, and the *maravedí*, a copper coin. The *ducado* was equal to 11 *reales* or 375 *maravedís*. The *escudo* was a gold coin also which replaced the *ducado* some time after 1537, although the *ducado* remained in circulation well into the seventeenth century. It was also equal to 11 *reales*. The really complicated coin was the *real*, equal to 34 *maravedís*, which had several variations, including *real de plata* and *de vellón*, the first of silver, the second a silver and copper alloy.[1] There was also an old copper coin, *una blanca* which was half the value of the *maravedí*, and another copper coin, *un cuarto*, equal to 4 *maravedís*. In the

---

1 To illustrate the difficulties of the multi-faceted *real*, which was equivalent to three old pennies, I give an example as late as 1736. An invoice totalling 328.25 *reales* was received by the rector of Salamanca from a merchant in Bilbao for goods in that year. He paid the bill in *reales de vellón*. He promptly received another copy of the same invoice with a revised total of 493 *reales* and 17 *maravedís*. The covering letter informed him that the first invoice had been given in *reales de plata* and as he was paying in *reales de vellón*; he now owed the difference between the two invoices (*Sal. Letters*, p. 6, 13/AA/38, 13/AA, 39). In 1915 Amelio Huarte wrote, 'taking into account the many circumstances that affect the value of money the *real* may be taken as two shillings approximately (of the currency in use in Ireland at the time). See 'Petitions of Irish students in the University of Salamanca 1574–1591' *Arch. Hib.* (1915), p. 98, fn. 2. As I mentioned, O'Doherty valued it as much less, i.e. two and a half pence: see footnote 16 in Chapter 1, above.

eighteenth century the *doblón* became the currency; it equalled 120 *reales*, and a variation, a *doblón sencillo,* was equal to 60 *reales.*

The *real* was the monetary unit used in the college ledger, together with the *maravedí.* In the book-keeping system of receipts and expenditure in the college, the amounts of money received, say, from the king, payable each month, was given in *reales* on the left hand side of the page and on the right hand side it was converted into *maravedís.* The books were balanced at each official visit.[2]

It was said at the time that the Jesuits were loath to take over the running of the Irish College in Santiago which had been first mooted in 1611. The reason was that they did not feel that the funding for the college was sufficient. In 1613 they were finally ordered to take it over without further ado. On 5 April 1613 the governor of Galicia, don Luís Henríquez, on orders from the king, handed over the seminary to the Society of Jesus and the *limosna* or grant of the king was paid for three months. The grant was to be 800 *reales* per month so the three months' grant of 2,400 *reales* was paid into the coffers of the college by the paymaster of the kingdom of Galicia, don Manuel de Espinosa. The royal grant was to sustain ten students and 200 *reales* were added to cover the maintenance of two priests of the Society of Jesus. Two other receipts are recorded, 510 *reales*, paid by two of the first students of the seminary after the takeover, Edward Hore and John Broder, towards their outfitting,[3] and the Chapter of Tui, *Cabildo de Tui*,[4] gave a grant of 60 *reales.* So the college started life with capital of roughly 2,970 *reales* and, as it was customary in the accounts to convert to *maravedís*, this is credited as 100,980 *maravedís.* There are 34 *maravedís* in one *real.* There were five items charged against this first receipt of funds in the period 5 April until the first official visit to the college by the provincial of Castile on 26 June 1613.[5] The items totalled 134,167 *maravedís*, leaving a debit balance of 3,187 *maravedís.* It seems that the college was set up with a debit balance and this was more or less its fate throughout its life.

2 The official visit was a feature of most of the Irish Colleges in Spain. See footnote 5.   3 Sal. Arch. 34/2, f. 5; the folios of this manuscript are numbered so I have given the numbers through-out. This is a bound volume entitled *Recibos* [receipts] *1622–1713*, amended to 1613–1713. The folios are numbered 2–144v, page 46 is blank and page 16 is missing. There is script on both sides of the folios. 4 The town of Tui, sometimes Tuy, south of Vigo is just over the border from Valença on the northern border of Portugal.   5 The college had an official visit,

The royal grant of 800 *reales* per month was a fixed amount and was paid on a regular basis, sometimes every three months, but at other times it might be in arrears for longer. At some stage it was paid in *tercios*, that is, in thirds or every four months. The second regular contribution came from the archbishop of Santiago who promised a fixed sum of fifty ducats a year. He also gave special grants at Christmas and Easter. Payments were received from time to time from other clerics, including the Cabildo de Santiago (the chapter) and the dean of Santiago. The queen gave a regular offering of 60 *reales* a month for masses of thanksgiving from 1613 until at least 1623.[6]

Other gifts were received on occasions; for instance, in 1618 an ornamental silver chalice and paten were presented to the college chapel by the chapter of Santiago; also a frontal, or altar hanging, was presented by the archbishop, Maximiliano, and a rose-coloured chasuble was given by the dean of S. Ciprian.[7] Individuals, both Irish and Spanish, contributed amounts of money to the college as alms, as well as giving mass offerings for the dead. The contributions of the students themselves, and in many cases their families, were very welcome and very necessary. In 1618 the college had funds of 5,000 *reales* which was the total of the deposits of the students in the house at the time. It appears that the students paid varying amounts for their maintenance, presumably whatever they could afford. They also brought funds to buy the articles of dress required for the Irish seminarians in Irish College. Since coins such as the ducat, or the doubloon, were either of gold or silver, they seemed to be interchangeable in different kingdoms. This is borne out by the fact that many of the students arriving from Ireland had in their possession a variety of coins for

sometimes every year, but more often than not there were longer gaps between visits (Sal. Arch. 34/2, f. 5). The next visit took place on 20 November 1616. The visitor was usually the provincial of the Jesuit order in Castile, to which Galicia belonged. We have details of several visits from June 1613 until 1713, mainly concerned with the examination of the college accounts from the date of the previous visit. The documents give recommendations by the visitors, not just about the finances, but about the running of the college in a general sense. Details of the visits will be given later in this chapter as they relate to life in the college. Jesuit Archives, Dublin, ICOL/SANT/3(1–20).   **6** The archbishop promised a fixed sum of 50 ducats a year: Sal. Arch. 34/2, f. 3. The dean of Santiago on one occasion in 1617 also gave a quantity of corn: Sal. Arch. 34/2, f. 3. The offering given for a mass was at this time 2 *reales*, so the queen's 60 *reales* a month covered one mass per day.   **7** Sal. Arch. 34/2, f. 10, 10v.

expenses. It is also recorded that they had rings or chains which could be converted into currency.[8]

There are many occasions when the Irish merchants in La Coruña, Bilbao and Bayona,[9] all important ports for trade with Ireland and Britain, contributed sums of money as alms to the college. There are also instances of the receipt of food from Ireland. In 1624 the rector, Thomas Briones, reports that 'De Irlanda embiaron alg.os amigos y otros irlandeses me dieron en Bayona dos barriles de manteca, un barril de lenguas de vacca saladas, unos quesos Irlandeses y otros cosillos para la casa' (From Ireland some friends and other Irish in Bayona gave me two barrels of butter, one barrel of salted cow-tongues, some Irish cheeses and other bits and pieces for the house).[10] On 26 December 1638 three students entered the

---

8 For instance, Archbishop James Lynch of Tuam wrote in June 1683 from Seville where he was then living to Richard Hore in La Coruña, who had been a student in Salamanca, requesting him to pass on to Jacomo Wigan & Co. a gold chain and two rings so that they might be disposed of to pay the outstanding debts of David Kirwan who had died prior to that date. *Sal. Letters*, p. 3, 13 AA 1 8a, 13 AA 1 9. 9 Bayona is a seaport west of Vigo. In the early years there are several mentions of Irish merchants giving contributions to the college. In 1616 three Irish merchants – John Fagan, Bayona, Gaspar White, Bilbao and Balthasar Aques (Waters?) – gave donations of 36, 20 and 8 *reales* respectively. It is noted that others also gave *varias cosas* (various things). Sal. Arch. 34/2, f. 10 v. A year later the sum of 75 *reales* was given by ten merchants, Patrick Levet, Dominick Browne, Vincent O'Brien, John Staffords, Peter Coppinger, Richard Enser, Gaspar White, Mark Comerford, Henry O'Neill and John Tyro: Sal. Arch. 34/2, f. 10 v. In 1624 the sum of 100 *reales* was donated by the Irish merchants in Bayona and a further 60 *reales* in the winter of the same year (Sal. Arch. 34/2, ff. 17, 18). Peter Englander, an Irish merchant in Bilbao, held 1,300 *reales* on behalf of three students (not named) and subsequently paid over to the college. Sal. Arch. 34/2, f. 21. 10 Sal. Arch. 34/2, f. 18. *Manteca* means lard or fat, and sometimes butter. Here it is probably butter; doubtless the cow-tongues are what we now call ox-tongues. Earlier the college received from friends in Ireland three cow hides, a barrel of salted salmon, a large pot of butter and a small one, with a dozen Irish cheeses: Sal. Arch. 34/2, f. 17. In December 1638 the students brought *medias* (wool socks or stockings) from Ireland and these were sold for 150 *reales*, ibid., f. 35. There was very little money in circulation in Ireland at this time so it would have been customary to give farm produce to the clergy and in general to pay in kind. The sending of quantities of food was a logical solution to a unique Irish problem. These could be sold for cash in the markets in Galicia. As there are seldom accents in Spanish mss of the time I have not included any in quotations, apart from the *tilde* over the ñ which is often included.

seminary, Andrew Kieron and Richard and John Burke, and brought 1,000 *reales* and a barrel of salmon which was sold for 150 *reales* and paid into the college coffers by the students. Another barrel of *manteca* was sold for 100 *reales* and also paid into the funds of the college.[11]

It seems that the college was also in the habit of selling off items, perhaps for ready cash, when there was a need, even to selling off food that might not last in storage. In July 1665 a dozen fish was sold for 32 *reales*, as the entry in the ledger tells us '*que se vendio porque se iva perdiendo*' (it was sold because it was going off). Other fish was also sold for 48 and a half *reales*, '*mas de setenta y siete libras de bacalao que se vendio por la misma razon*' (more that seventy-seven pounds of cod was sold for the same reason).[12] *Una olla de manteca de puerca que se perdia y se vendio a los zurradores* was sold for 11 *reales* (a pot of pork fat which was sold to the tanners for 11 *reales* as it, too, was going off). Three pounds of surplus sugar and a half *ferrado* of beans were also sold in 1655. There is even an occasion in 1665 when things must have been very straitened indeed: an old cape, belonging to one of the students, was sold for 70 *reales*.[13]

The accounts, which were closely scrutinised by the visiting provincial, give many unexpected insights into the financial management and running of the establishment and also, unexpectedly, the names of students who paid in money for their maintenance (called *alimentos* or food), and for their outfitting (*vestuario*). The outfitting of each student included the buying of the required materials and the engaging of the services of a tailor to make their clerical garb. Sometimes this cost increased by an overtime payment to the tailor who worked into the night to finish an urgent order. Shoes had to be handmade also by a cobbler, and various supplies had to be bought for each student, paper, inkwell, *vade, petrina*[14] and portfolio.

A *costurera*, seamstress, was also employed by the college to make shirts for the collegians and to do mending and repair work on their clothes which of necessity had to last a long time and were often handed down to future collegians. The seamstress also made new collars for old shirts when

---

11 Sal. Arch. 34/2, f. 34v.　**12** Ibid., f. 67v.　**13** Sal. Arch. 34/2, ff. 52, 67v. The *ferrado* was an old corn-measure. Leather workers used oils and animal fats to curry hides to make them pliable or to strengthen them.　**14** *Vade* or *Vademecum*, a notebook. Luís Cortés Vázquez in *La vida estudiantil en la Salamanca clásica* (Salamanca, 1996), p. 173 describes it as a kind of leather folder which students carry and holds the notes they take down in the schools; *petrina*, pertaining to or written by the apostle Peter.

they were worn out. The *costurera*, like the washerwoman, the barber (who was also the *sangrador* or blood-letter) and the doctor was paid an annual fee. She was supplied with the cloth for the shirts but had to supply the thread herself.[15]

An example of a typical account for a student may be of interest. I have selected one at random, that of Richard Lincoln who was later archdeacon of Glendalough and archbishop of Dublin from 1755 to 1763. He arrived in the college on 8 June 1724 to start his course. He was debited with various sums in the college ledger for his outfit and his maintenance from 8 June to 18 October, that is for 132 days, at the rate of 3 *reales* per day. The total cost for his maintenance was 396 *reales*. He cleared all these charges by handing over *un doblón de a ocho*, worth 240 *reales*, some silver coins, worth 150 *reales*, 300 *reales*, 210 *reales*, and *un doblón sencillo* equal to 50 *reales*. There is no date indicating when his payment was made. His final deposit added up to a total of 960 *reales*.[16] The items for his clothing were:

8 *varas*[17] of blue woollen cloth at 20 *reales* a *vara* for his *veca* or sash	160 reales	
2 and one third *varas* of fine cloth of Segovia at 38 *reales* a vara for the *chupa*[18]	88 rrs	22 mrs[19]
un bonete y cruz (a tippet and cross)	12 rrs	
6 and a half *varas* of black serge at 9 rrs a *vara*	58 rrs	17 mrs
I *vara* of brown Holland fine linen	4 rrs	17 mrs
I half *vara* of buckram, 2 and a half *varas* of silk thread, hooks and eyes, tapes	II rrs	17 mrs
2 and a half *varas* of linen for lining	7 rrs	17 mrs
the making of the *beca* by the tailor	6 rrs	
2 pairs of shoes	27 rrs	
3 and a half *varas* of *sempiterna*[20] to line the *chupa*	24 rrs	17 mrs
another pair of shoes	13 rrs	
charge for credit for this balance[21]	150 rrs	29 mrs
maintenance for 132 days mentioned above	396 rrs	
Total	960 rrs	

15 She was paid 33 *reales* for the year ending October 1669. In 1667 she was paid an extra 9 *reales* for ironing albs and corporals. The doctor was paid 100 *reales* each year and the *barbero/ sangrador* 80 *reales* per year: Sal. Arch. XXIV/1,34/7. In 1667 the barber/bloodletter, Juan Romero, was paid his salary half yearly. **16** Sal. Arch. 34/7. **17** The *vara* was an old measure of about 2.8 feet, the *veca* or *beca* was a long sash worn by college students around the neck and reaching to the feet.

The seminarian was dressed completely in black, except for his sash of blue; he wore an under-coat with sleeves, also black, as was the tippet on his head. All wore the cross on the chest and probably a cloak in inclement weather.[22]

I have already mentioned the official visits to the college. The main thrust of these was to inspect the account books of the college which listed receipts and payments since the previous official visit. In the process a great deal of detailed information is written into the ledgers which is of great importance in the building up of a picture of life in the college. In all I have found records of over 38 visits during the period 1613–1713.[23] Apart from the facts about financial matters of the college during its first hundred years there is also some colourful information on sources of income. The comments of the visitors include their views on conditions in the college, advice to the rector on various questions, recommendations and, occasionally, praise as well as criticisms. The first visit took place in June 1613, only two months after the Society of Jesus took over the administration of the college.

On 14 June 1618 the Provincial, P. Diego de Sossa, refers to matters raised during the 1614 visit, details of which I have not seen.[24] The report of this earlier visit apparently laid down the ground rules of the local Jesuit college and included the assertion that the rector of the Irish College was to be subject and subordinate to the rector of the Jesuit College in Santiago. It specified that the Irish College should not engage in lawsuits, must not buy real estate without prior communication and was not to undertake any building, even student bedrooms.

Visitors in 1641, 1668 and 1674 were loud in their praise of the good atmosphere prevailing in the college. Fr Antonio Velazquez in 1641 asserted that he found much edification in the house. Fr Diego de la Fuente de Hurtado in 1674 tells us that he spoke individually to each student and

18 The *chupa* was an undercoat with sleeves. 19 The abbreviations used in documents for *reales* and *maravedís* are *rrs.* and *mrs.* 20 This was a type of serge. 21 He was, in addition, charged the hefty sum of 150 *reales* and 29 *maravedís* in what appears to be a charge for credit. 22 A print of the costume of a student of the Irish College, Salamanca which would have been similar to that of a student of the Irish College, Santiago, is reproduced in Agnes Neligan (ed.), *Maynooth Library treasures* (Dublin, 1995), p. 113. It is by Revd Bradford, engraved by I. Clark, aquatint with water colour wash published by J. Booth, London, 1809. 23 Irish Jesuit Archives, Dublin, ICOL/SANT/3(1–20), *Visitatio Collegii Hibernorum Compostellani.* 24 So far I have not found details of this particular visit. The financial details are generally from the Sal. Arch. 34/2.

found the rules and the constitution were being adhered to.[25] He also noted the peace and goodness in the house, and said the students were exemplary and attentive to their studies. The 1668 visitor, Fr Antonio Gonzalvez, found the seminary very 'pacifico, exemplar y atento a sus estudios y obligaciones' (peaceful, exemplary and attentive to study and obligations). He also remarked that, as usual, there is much concern with shortage of money. As well as these complimentary remarks there is also high praise from two of the visitors of the rector, Andrew Lynch (1669–94), who was probably the longest-serving Irish rector there.

Another endorsement of the college is evidenced by the fact that the archbishop of Santiago thought highly enough of it to enrol his nephew in 1723 there as a boarder, un convictor. This was from 21 May 1723 until 18 October, for 149 days at a cost of 447 reales. Also on two occasions the archbishop's young gentlemen pages, sus cavalleros pajes,[26] were lodged in the college as paying guests, four of them for 365 days in 1723 and in 1724/5 five pages for 287 days, costing 4,380 reales and 4,305 reales respectively. These amounts, totalling 9,132 reales, were paid over the years 1724 and 1725 in six instalments.[27]

Some of the local rules singled out for mention are of interest. In 1634 the visitor, P. Alonso del Caño, was concerned that the door in the Irish College chapel which led into the hallway and onto the street should be kept shut and no services should be administered there to people from the outside. What the reason for this prohibition or what kind of services were being administrated I have not been able to ascertain. In that year the college was already established in no. 44 Rua Nueva, the main door of the college opened onto the street; there was also a door at the back of the college which led into Rua Vilar where there was a laneway. However, in a memorial of complaints against the Society of Jesus with regard to the administration of the Irish Colleges in Spain sent by the students to Philip IV in 1642, the complaint did surface that they were forbidden to exercise any pastoral ministry with the local people.[28]

25 His is the only report which mentions the fact that he had spoken individually to the students.   26 Being a page to the archbishop of Santiago was a signal honour. It meant that these young boys were from noble houses and took part in the frequent ceremonial processions in the cathedral city. In fact, the elaborate nature and splendour of the ceremonies in Santiago must have been at odds with the underground church in Ireland and must have given much thought to the collegians during their years there.   27 Sal. Arch. 34/7. The cost per day was 3 reales. 28 Rivera, op. cit., pp 429–30. See Chapter 6 regarding this memorial.

Four years later on 4 June 1638 the same visitor, Alonso del Caño, warned that *estudiantes vagabundos*, wandering students, should not be admitted to the seminary, nor should any of them be allowed to study the course except students sent by the Provincial in Ireland. He also emphasised that the Irish provincial should be informed of this rule in writing. Furthermore, students sent must be selected from all the provinces of Ireland. This was also ordered by the visitor in 1687, who complained that of the eight students in the college three were from one province, two from another, two from yet another and there was only one from Munster. Unfortunately, he does not name the provinces of the other seven. He emphasises that His Majesty's orders regarding students being received equally from the four provinces of Ireland must be adhered to.[29]

In 1668 Fr Antonio González also advises that no more students should be taken in than can be comfortably accommodated. This advice is repeated on many other occasions. For example, the official visitor in 1676 maintained that individuals who come from Ireland should not be admitted at the expense of the seminary and should rather wait until the Arts students had left for Salamanca in April or June or else until the course was about to begin in October. This visitor, P. Diego de la Fuente Hurtado, was concerned that eight new entrants were awaiting entry to study Arts, and the seminary would scarcely have resources to maintain those who were finishing their course that year. There were, of course, also difficulties in Salamanca to receiving those ready to start theology. This is another case of the overlap of one group of students finishing and another waiting to gain entry.

On several occasions the visitors were 'adamant that students should not linger in the college once they finished their course', and he ordered that they should leave immediately for Salamanca when their third (and later second) arts course was completed. Clearly, this order was based on economics. The college could only sustain a certain number of students and, if there was an overlap, even for a few weeks as the next batch arrived it caused a serious financial strain. There are lots of instances of criticisms also coming from Salamanca about receiving students from Santiago for the same reason and also without due notice.

The visitor in 1638 pointed out that every year at the end of the course examiners from the Jesuit College who tested their own brethren and also examined the Irish College students drew attention to those found to be

29 *Visitatio Collegii Hibernorum Compostellani*, Jesuit Archives ICOL/SANT/3 (1).

unfit for the course of study. The visitor was of the opinion that those thus categorised should be expelled and that efforts to keep numbers to a sustainable level should be made as long as the royal grants were often in an uncertain state. It was stressed that the college should not find itself again in straits similar to those of other years when it was not able to meet its debts.

The visitor in July 1686 was concerned about a novelty that had been introduced into the seminary by the students who now had *llaves particulares* (individual keys) for their bedrooms (*aposentos*), and the superior consequently was not free to visit their rooms when he judged it necessary. The verdict was that the rector must arrange to have a key to open all doors.

The following year the visitor, Juan Nieto, advised the rector, Andrew Lynch, to share out equally *los oficios de algun trabajo*, the duties of some set tasks, and if students failed to carry out the tasks the punishment should be equal also.

A rather surprising note is added by P. Antonio de Ybarra on 1 October 1660 giving instructions that guests should not be received in the seminary and that those that did visit should only be received for the time that Christian charity requires. He adds an admonition that the students should study more, not miss lectures or go out of the college too often and when they do they should always be accompanied by a named companion. He also advises that more penances should be given out when necessary.

Six years later the same subject of Irish visitors to the college is condemned by the visitor, Miguel de Arbiza, as causing loss of time without benefit to the students. 'Tambien le ruego al Pe. Rector que continue con el cuidado que tiene de estorvar que entren y traten en el seminario los sujetos de su Nacion que pueden causar perdida de tiempo sin provechos de los Alumnos y con daño de lo temporal, como hasta aquí lo ha ejecutado' (I also ask the rector to continue to obstruct visits of his fellow countrymen to the college which are without benefit to the pupils and cause loss of time as has happened up to now). Jeremiah Sweetman was rector at the time. Whether other rectors ignored this particular order or not, I do not know.

In July 1686 P. Andrés Reguera described the account books as showing 'their income in a pitiful, bankrupt state' (*sus rentas en tan lastimosa quiebra*) with only 561 *reales* left. He even suggested that the students would have to write home to see if funds for food could be secured from Ireland. Two years later the same Provincial, Andres Reguera, affirms that all the seminaries, including Salamanca, are in very bad financial shape and have either lost all their income or have been left with very little. Presumably, the college borrowed heavily from other Jesuit houses or from local people prepared to make loans to them. In fact, in the 1680s the students are recorded as paying 635 *reales* for their food '*por q. el seminario no cobran sus rentas*' (because the seminary is not receiving its income). This was by order of the provincial.[30]

There follows a gap of four years before the next visit. From 1686 until 1692, seven long lean years for the seminaries, the grants were in arrears. Perhaps these 'lean years' were exacerbated by the war in Ireland (1688–92) when funds in Ireland were needed to sustain the Jacobite cause. In 1692 P. Antonio Caraveo made a visit and we have the happy news that the arrears, totalling 64,800 *reales*, have finally been paid. This was roughly 9,257 *reales* for each of the years left unpaid.

Details of the food consumed in the Irish College may be gleaned from the lists of provisions which the visitors found and listed in their reports. They provide information into the practical side of life in the college. The early visitors stated that little or no provisions were held by the college. In 1614 the visitor found '*no tiene el colegio provisiones algunas sino un poco de vino*' (the college has no provisions except a little wine). In 1626 it was noted that '*tiene el seminario vino para el año q. viene*' (the seminary has enough wine for a year) and in 1654 '*no tiene el sem.o al presente provisiones ningunas de importancia*' (the seminary has not at present provisions of any importance). Over the years, however, by some means they managed to secure sizeable quantities of some essential foodstuffs and other commodities. From 1654 on, the position regarding provisions improved and supplies of wheat and wine were stored in the college. Sometimes the visitor reported that stocks of these were held and also that candles for a year were often held. The wine and candles were particularly important for the celebration of mass. In this connection it is interesting to note that the Irish Franciscans when they first arrived in Louvain, being very poor and not having a place to celebrate mass in their cloister, were refused permission to say mass in the parish church because the clergy there could not afford to supply the candles and wine for the services. Times were hard and every penny counted in the survival of the parish clergy.[31]

---

30 Sal. Arch. 34/2, f. 90v.   31 See Fr Adam Hamilton OSB, *The chronicle of the English Augustinian Canonesses Regular of the Lateran at St Monica's in Louvain* (Edinburgh and London, 1904), i, pp 71–2, quoted by Fr Cathaldus Giblin OFM, 'Hugh McCaghwell,OFM, archbishop of Armagh (+ 1626). Aspects of his life'

As time went on, stocks of bacon, wax, candles, honey, nuts, vinegar, beans, onions, peppers, saffron, fruit, sugar, salt and raisins are recorded, indicating that the college was well integrated into Spanish eating and drinking habits. Also in the lists of provisions noted by the college visitors property such as copper pots and other kitchen utensils were included as valuables. Blankets, linen, table napkins were also given a valuation, on one occasion totalling 1,835 *reales*. In fact, in 1676 the provisions held were valued at 3,090 *reales* and included oil, wheat, 5 *moyos of wine* (a *moyo* had a capacity of 258 litres), wax, hay, bacon and sugar.[32]

There were two servants in the college at all times, one being a *criado de cocina* (a kitchen servant), perhaps the cook, who was paid 6 ducats a year in 1764. On 21 January 1768 the *criado de cocina*, Gregorio de Sylva, was given the money to buy a pair of shoes. Cooks did not last long in colleges, and Gregorio was no exception. The laconic note in the ledger is that he escaped from the college when paid on 1 March 'con menoscabo de la casa y de otros sujetos' (to the detriment of the house and of other individuals).[33]

From an early stage in its history the college owned a number of houses in Santiago from which some income was generated. Documents in the Salamanca Archives relating to these properties include a list of the *bienes* and *rentas* (properties and income) dated 1752 and an inventory of legal documents dated 1873.[34] Knowledge of the complex system of ownership of houses and lands in Spain, with various obligations attached, is well outside my limited field of expertise. Some of the houses were formerly church-owned and apparently carried obligations of various kinds which involved the duty of saying a certain number of masses, and others involved payments of *dominios*, that is, legal fees imposed on the properties.

The earlier list was compiled by the Spanish rector of the Irish College, Diego Araujo SJ (1735–64), who was ordered by the superior in Santiago to compile a report on the goods and income of the college. In September 1752 he presented this document, giving details of the properties and

Sea. AM 11:2, 1985, p. 269, fn. 22.   **32** Sal. Arch. 34/2, f. 84.   **33** Sal. Arch. 34/7. **34** Sal. Arch. 33/1/1–2. The 1873 inventory was held by the Salamanca college after the college had taken over the property of the Santiago college. Some of the documents are no longer amongst the archival material in Maynooth. This is not surprising as most of the properties were eventually disposed of either in the years after the college was incorporated into the Irish College, Salamanca in 1767 or before the affairs of Salamanca were wound up prior to its closure in the 1950s.

income of the college and this included seven houses. These were all *casas aforadas* (leased houses) and appear to have been in the possession of the college in the early seventeenth century.

Two of these, one with two upper floors and the other with one, in the calle Entrehornos, parish of Sta Salomé, had an annual rent of 300 and 120 *reales* respectively. Both of these houses were bought in 1621. In the later seventeenth century, 1676 and 1678, the college was still receiving rent for these two houses. In the ledger they are referred to eventually as houses one and two. It appears that one of these houses was given to the college in payment of an outstanding debt. Another house was in the calle de Pregontoiro, parish of S. Benito, and was acquired in 1717, a fourth house was in the parish of S. Gines near the Jesuit house, the last three were in the parish of Santa María la Real de Sar, one in the calle de Sta María de Sar, which had a small piece of land, and another house attached to it, also with a patch of land; and the last one was near *'fuente de S. Nicolás'*.[35]

The inventory, dated 1873, cited above mentions eight houses, apparently the same houses in the calle de Entrehornos; now the parish is given as the same as the college, the third house is in the calle de Preguntoiro and the parish is now given as 'S. Felix de Solario', with another with one upper floor in the calle Fuente Seca, acquired in 1693. Apart from these, which appear to have been suitable to rent, there were four houses in the calle de S. Nicolás, parish of Sta María la Real de Sar, which are described as 'quasi ynavitables pr un riachuelo que pasa pr dentro de una de ellas, se suforaron a Dn Joan Farina con la pen.on de catorce ducados y de ellos paga el colegio a Dn Ign.o Cajam.o o al Illm.o Cavildo de Sant.o cada ano ciento quince rr. diez y ocho mr. como tanvien cinco rr. al rector de Sn Benito del Campo de esta ciu.d. limosna de dos misas fundadas en dha Parroquia S.re las mismas casas' (also uninhabitable because of a stream which passed through one of them, rented to D. Joan Farina at a rent of 14 ducats from which the college pays 115 *reales* 18 *maravedís* every year to D. Ignacio Cajamiento or to the Chapter of Santiago, also 5 *reales* 18 *maravedís* to the rector of S. Benito del Campo of this city for two masses founded in said parish on the said houses). It is further explained that as this property was 'ruined and uninhabitable for many years and derelict with other ruined buildings in the tenancy of Sar; it was labelled as such because of being in an area of little esteem.' Because of the condition of this property the annual rent was a bare 33 *reales*.[36]

35 Sal. Arch. 33/1/1.   **36** Ibid.

There was also a house in the calle de la Barroira, La Coruña, which was donated to the college in 1672 by the Revd Thomas Kiernan. The circumstances of this donation are not clearly defined in any records I found. In January 1664 *Da. Francisca de Quinones*, widow of D. *Bartolome Lopez de Figueros* and her son, *D. Alvaro Lopez* sold to '*Thomas Quirano, clérigo irlandes, una placa sita en la calle de la Barroira, La Coruña*' (Thomas Kier(n)an, an Irish cleric, a site in the calle de Barroira, La Coruña) which had been a house, then tumbled down, for 500 *reales*. Fr Kiernan built a new house on the site, '*una casa alta de sobrado nuevo que el mismo hizo y edifico sita en la rua de Barreira de la Peccadaria*' (a high house, with a new attic, which he himself built in the rua de Barreira de la Peccadaria).

On 4 May 1668 *Francisca de Estrada* sold him 'por la mitad de la plazuela territorio que esta en la calle de la Barreira de Peccaderia unida a la anterior a precio de 94 rrs' (for half of the little square which is in the calle de la Barreira de la Peccadaria, joined to (his house) for 94 *reales*).[37]

This house carried some sort of obligation which the college paid when they were given ownership of it at a later stage. Fr Kiernan made a gift of it to the college in 1672. Subsequently, in March 1684, the rector, Andrew Lynch SJ, leased it to Francisco de Candas.[38]

In 1682 the college received 100 *reales* as rent on another house inherited in La Coruña.[39] The college was also liable to pay to the Royal Hospital (now the *parador*) an annual amount of 4 *reales*, which appears to be a *foro* or rental attached to this house. There are receipts for this payment for the years 1656 to 1660, 1661 to 66, and 1672 to 1675.[40]

From time to time details appear of other financial arrangements which the Irish College had and which yielded income. These were *censos* and *juros*. The Jews, who traditionally were the royal moneylenders, were expelled from Spain in 1492. Spain then became deeply indebted to foreign bankers, mainly Genoese, but also Flemish and German. From the mid-sixteenth century well into the seventeenth, the state strove to balance its books by floating various other loans, including the *juros*, which were loans to the crown introduced in the form of annuities. The amount borrowed was repaid with interest over several years until the debt was cleared (in the fifteenth century 10 per cent was paid but over time the interest rate became lower and lower).[41]

---

37 Ibid. 38 Ibid. Both spellings *Barroira* and *Barreira* appear. 39 Sal. Arch. 34/2, f. 90 v. 40 Sal. Arch. XXIV/1. 41 See Henry Kamen, *Spain, 1469–1714* (London, 1991); also *Spain in the later seventeenth century, 1665–1700* (London, 1980).

The grant of 9,600 *reales* paid annually to the college by royal order was based on a *juro* which came from the hated sales tax, the *alcabala*. This tax, of Moorish origin, was levied on almost everything. So the college grant came ultimately from the taxes collected in Galicia from this levy. The clergy were exempted from many taxes and there were in the college accounts examples of refunds (*refacciónes*) on tax paid on meat by the college to the *carnecería pública* (the public butcher market).

The *censo* was also a kind of annuity but these loans were made by individuals or municipalities and again were repayable with interest until the debt was eliminated. The college held several of these, some for small sums. However, it appears that repayment on these were often in arrears. For example, the *censos* belonging to the college were listed in 1769 and many of them were unpaid. The income on one, called 'Duque de Medinacoeli' was reported then to be unpaid since 1767 as were most of the others, one being three years in arrears. They were known by various names – *Onel, de Arines, de Olla, Moimenta* and so on.[42]

The college for a time had an arrangement with a Fr Luís Arguelles who was a collector of charitable donations, referred to as *obra pia* (pious works). This *obra pia* did yield some cash in the 1680s when money was scarce in the college. There is also another document of contract between rector Richard Conway, the Irish in Santiago and a Fr Froylán Alonso García, a native of Sotillo de Sanbría, in the diocese of Lugo. This man was empowered to collect the *petitorio* (petitions) for all the churches and parishes of the archbishopric and its suffragan bishoprics and sought alms for the seminary in September 1627 when the college had to seek what was termed *socorros* or assistance. A fifteenth of what was collected went to the official collector.[43]

In the 1680s the college invested 9,000 *reales* with Philip Stafford and this yielded a *lucro*, or dividend, of 7 per cent. Philip Stafford appears to have been on close terms with the Irish College. He lived in La Coruña and was consul of England and Ireland. Originally he was referred to as consul of the kingdom of Ireland as well as England; later he was referred to as consul of the kingdom of England and the provinces of Ireland. Later still this was reduced to simply 'consul of England' and he was described as '*consul de S. M. Británnica en la Coruña*'. His son, Nicholas, was lodged in the college for some time '*a cursarse siendo novicio*' (to study, being a novice). He appears to have been a novice or freshman studying for entry

42 Sal. Arch. 33/1/1.   **43** Sal. Arch. 34/2, f. 90v; Couselo, op. cit., p. 13.

into the Society of Jesus and is often referred to as *hermano* (brother) Stafford. His father paid the college for his board and lodging.[44]

One of the most interesting and unusual sources of income of the Irish College was the right to a *maradeví* on every *ferrado* of produce sold in the Alhóndiga, the public granary of the city of Santiago. In 1689 Philip Stafford bought the *derechos* (rights) of the Alhóndiga at auction and later sold them to the Irish College on 27 July 1699 for 11,000 *reales*. He had the right to a *blanca* (or half a *maravedí*) on every *ferrado* of grain sold in the market, 'el derecho de blanca, en ferrado y medio ferrado de la medicion de granos de la Alhóndiga de la Placa de esa ciudad de Santiago' (the right to a *blanca* on a *ferrado* and half *ferrado* of the measurment of grain in the cornmarket of this city of Santiago). The college got one *maravedí*, so he did slightly better.[45] The college got a good income from this investment for many years until the suppression of the Jesuits. It was then taken over by the Ayuntamiento.

At the time of the suppression the Irish College, Santiago was subsumed into the Irish College, Salamanca, and its assets should have gone to the latter college. The authorities in Salamanca which was by then ruled by secular rectors, made several attampts to get this *derecho* back. Their legal advisers made the point that the rights had not been given to the college by royal grant or by the Ayuntamiento in ancient times but by formal sale and purchase and consequently the Ayuntamiento was exceeding its faculties by being judge and party. They emphasised that the right had been purchased by the college for cash and the right to the income had been enjoyed by them since that time. In the reign of Isabel II (1843–68) the government suppressed 'los oficios o cargos de fiel medida y libertando a los pueblos de estos grabamenes y proponiendo el medio de indemniar a los actuales poseedores' (the offices and duties of accurate measurement and proposing the relief of the people from these burdens and a way of indemnifying the present owners [of the rights]. It does not appear that the Irish College, Salamanca got any satisfactory result in spite of all the legal arguments of their advisers.[46]

Donal O'Sullivan Beare lived in Galicia for some time, his main residence being in Valença, near the Portuguese border, before transferring to Madrid (where the court was) from 1606. He was murdered there in 1618, his assassin being Sir John Bathe, whom he had befriended and who

---

44 Sal. Arch. 34/2, f. 92.   **45** Sal. Arch. 33/1/1–2.   **46** Sal. Arch. 33/1/2.

was said to have been a double agent.[47] After his death the ownership of a house which had been granted apparently to both the college and to the count of 'Biraven' [Beerhaven] was the subject of litigation between the college and the countess, his widow, and his son.[48] She was granted the house, and the college waived its rights to possession of it. An amicable settlement was made. This was apparently one of the royal houses mentioned earlier which the college had probably occupied for a time before the house on the Rua Nova was bought in 1618.

The college was closed down in 1767 on the suppression of the Jesuits and the house was eventually sold in 1770 for 107,806 *reales*.[49] It was reported at that time that the income of the college was made up of 9 per cent from *censos*, 7 per cent from the rents on five houses and 11.8 per cent from the returns on the Alhóndiga. The balance was based on the royal grants and various *limosnas*.

47 The authorities wanted O'Sullivan dead. He was determined to continue the struggle. The Bathes were the family who lived in the estate in Drumcondra, Dublin which is now occupied by the residence of the Catholic archbishop of Dublin. Dr Downey suggests that John Bathe's brother, or kinsman, Fr William (?) Bathe SJ tried to turn the college in Santiago into a seminary contrary to the wishes of O'Sullivan-Beare. **48** Elena, Condesa de Biraven was Eileen O'Sullivan, daughter of O'Sullivan Mor and his wife Maria Carthy. Her brother, Daniel O'Sullivan Mor came to Spain with Donal Cam in 1604. Her younger son, Dermicio, later married into one of the most important aristocratic families in Spain. His wife was doña Mariana de Cardona y Córdoba y Aragón, grand-daughter of the Duque de Sesa, don Antonio de Cardona y Córdoba, Gran Almirante of Naples during the reign of Philip II (Sal. Arch. 27/9). Dermicio had been a page at court after the death of his elder brother and subsequently in 1613 a Knight of Santiago. Donal Cam himself was admitted to the Order of Santiago a year before his untimely death. Micheline Kerney Walsh, 'O'Sullivan Beare; some unpublished documents XLV', *Arch. Hib.* pp 45, 51, 58; *Knights*, i, pp 1–2, 4–6. See Denis O'Doherty, 'Domnal O'Sullivan Beare and his family in Spain', *Studies*, 19 (1930), pp 211–26. **49** Castelao, op. cit., p. 98.

CHAPTER 4

Rectors

The Society of Jesus was responsible for the administration of the Irish College in Santiago de Compostela from 1613 until the suppression of the order in 1767 in the kingdom of Spain. In official Jesuit documents, rectors of the college were often referred to as superiors, whereas the Irish generally called them rectors. The dates of the duration of rectorships in the college which I include here are in many cases tentative. The available records are frequently unclear and sometimes contradictory.[1] In the list I give in this chapter there are over-laps, as rectors were appointed at times for a few months at the end of a year or acted for some time at the beginning in some cases. Where possible, I have sought for definitive documentation, for example, internal evidence, but, alas, this is not always available.

As the Jesuits were the administrators of the Santiago college it may be useful to explain the organisational features of the Jesuit system and perhaps trace briefly the origins of the Society or *Compañia* as it was called in Spanish. Founded in 1539 by St Ignatius Loyola it was conceived as a community of well-educated priests bound by their vows of obedience, poverty and chastity and the strict rules formulated by St Ignatius. He had been a soldier before his conversion and subsequent entry into the spiritual life in his new religious order. It was an order differing in many ways from the existing orders of the church.[2]

---

1 For information on the rectors the following documents were consulted:– Jesuit Archives, Dublin and include ICOL/Sant/1, 2, 3, 5, 'A Biographical Dictionary of the Irish Jesuits in the time of the Society's third Irish Mission 1598–1773,' ed. Fr Francis Finnegan SJ; Catálogos públicos de la provincia de Castilla del año de 1597–1600, Cat. MSS. Hib. SJ three volumes (1556–1755). Documents in the Salamanca Archives in NUI, Maynooth (Russell Library) and articles published in *Archivium Hibernicum* and *Irish Ecclesiastical Record*. In this chapter I have listed the rectors in chronological order, followed by short biographical notes on each.   2 The main innovation was the abolition of the breviary or office in choir. For the new order the office was to be said privately. The principles of the Society of Jesus were to form churchmen, not only in natural goodness but also of firm character and obedience and submission to the commands of the superior. The

The theory of St Ignatius was that there was a state of war following the Protestant revolt in the sixteenth century against the Church of Rome. The Society of Jesus was founded twenty-two years after Luther nailed his ninety-five theses to the door of the Church of All Saints in the university city of Wittenberg on 1 November 1517 or nineteen years after his burning of the papal bull excommunicating him on 10 December 1520. St Ignatius Loyola adopted a military approach to halt the advance of attackers in the train of Luther and the other reformers.[3] The pope, Paul III, on 27 September 1540 in his bull of licence for the new Society gave it a military name *Regimini militantis ecclesiae* (Guide for soldiers of the church, or those willing to fight for the church of God).[4]

The head of the Society was the General in Rome who enjoyed complete authority in the organisation which was divided into Provinces wherever Jesuit houses were founded. The Society of Jesus in its beginnings in the Iberian peninsula consisted of one province, namely Hispania, which included Spain and Portugal. Later it was divided into many more provinces – Aragon, Castile and so on – and this process went on until there were further divisions over the years and by the time of the suppression of the Society by the pope in 1773 there were forty-one provinces throughout the world.[5]

On entering the Society, students were sent for two years to one of the Jesuit colleges to study philosophy and often to another college to study theology for a further two years. For example, Fr Conway, the first Jesuit rector of the Irish College in Santiago de Compostela, followed a two-year philosophy course in the college in Monterey and then studied theology for a further two years at the Royal College in Salamanca. The candidate wishing to become a Jesuit went through various stages – novice, scholastic, temporary coadjutor (lay brother), spiritual coadjutor – and finally was professed of three or four vows. In the Irish Colleges priests on the staff all had their own titles – rector, *socius* (advisor), *procurador* (bursar), *operarius* (worker) and minister, each with well-defined duties.

General of the Society was in a position of complete authority and was likened to a general of a secular army commander at war.   **3** In the words of St Ignatius 'The society shall adapt itself to the times and not the times to the society': *Encyclopaedia Britannica*, 13th ed., vols 15/16 (1926), p. 342. See contributions on the Jesuits by RFL and E.Tn – Rev. Richard Frederick Littledate (1833–1890) and Rev. Ethelred Luke Taunton (d.1907) – in the same volume, pp 337–47.   **4** Ibid., p. 343.   **5** In the provinces of the Society the usual institutions were novitiate, colleges, professed houses and mission houses. The teaching mission of the Jesuits was of paramount importance with *ratio studiorum* playing a central part.

Rectors of Irish College Santiago de Compostela
1605–1767

Eugene MacCarthy	1605–13	Andrew Lincoln	1660–6[11]
Richard Conway	1613–19	Jeremiah Sweetman	1666–8
Thomas White	1619–22	Andrew Lynch	1668/9–94
William White	1622 ?[6]	Antonius López	1694–5
Thomas Briones	1622–4[7]	Barnaby Bathe	1695–1710[12]
Paul Sherlock[8]	1624–8	Antonius de Cangas	1710–11
Nicholas White	1628[9]	Juan de Mondragón	1712
Thadeus O'Sullivan	1629–31	James O'Connor Henriques	1712–24
James Carney (O Kearney)	1631–46	John Henriques (Harrison)	1724–8
Peter Reid	1647–8	Didacus de Araujo	1729–64
Ignatius Lombard	1648–52[10]	Santiago de Ayuso	1764–7
Christoval Acuña	1652–3	Pedro Rodríquez[13]	1767
William Salinger	1653–60	Patricio Kenney[14]	1767–9

6 Some sources mention William White as rector in 1623, e.g. Sal. Arch. 34/2, f. 17 says in 1623 'Aquí comença el Padre Guillermo Vitus' (here commences William White), presumably as rector. **7** Fr Finnegan, 'Irish rectors at Seville, 1619–1687', 5th series *IER*, 106 (1966), pp 50–1, indicates that he was rector there in September 1623. Another source, Sal. Arch. 34/2, f. 14v, states 1622 'desde aquí começo el P. Thomas Briones' (from here Thomas Briones began). According to William McDonald's list of Salamanca rectors, *IER*, xi (1874), pp 113–14 Briones was rector in Salamanca from 1613 to 1631. However, according to O'Doherty (*Arch. Hib.*, 3 (1914) p. 95) the rector in Salamanca in 1623–5 was Fr P. Comorton. Paul Sherlock tells us in his autobiography that he was about to leave for Ireland when ordered to take up the rectorship in Santiago around Easter of 1624. **9** Nicholas White is another possible rector who may have acted for a short period between the departure of Paul Sherlock and the start of Thadeus O'Sullivan's rectorship. **10** He left on 8 January 1652, Sal. Arch. 34/2, f. 43. **11** Fr Lincoln is listed as rector in Salamanca, 1665–89, by McDonnell, op. cit., p. 114. **12** Fr Bathe is given as rector in Salamanca, 1693–6, by McDonnell, op. cit., p. 114. **13** Fr Rodríquez was the parish priest of the church of Sta María Salomé; he was a secular priest (this was the time of the suppression of the Jesuits in Spain). Couselo, op. cit., p. 17. **14** Fr Kenney was *Confesor de lenguas* (confessor in various languages) in the Cathedral, Santiago. He was appointed rector when Fr Rodríguez was dismissed. Couselo, op. cit., p. 17.

BIOGRAPHICAL NOTES

The first rector of the college was a secular priest, Fr Eugene Kilian MacCarthy, who had been parish priest of Fermoy, Co. Cork, diocese of Cloyne. He came to the continent in 1602 after the edict of expulsion from Ireland. T.J.Walsh[15] quotes from a pamphlet, published in Bordeaux in 1619, by Diarmuid MacCarthy, founder of the Irish College in Bordeaux (1603–1793), listing the names of Irish priests who found refuge in Bordeaux at that time. He cites 'Pere Eugenius Cartaeus du diocese de Cluanen, abbe de Fermoy, qui a este superior du College Hibernois dix ou douze ans a St Jacques de Gallice'. He was probably related to the rector of Bordeaux and at some stage made his way to Santiago and organised an educational centre there for the Irish exiles prior to the setting up of the Irish College in 1605.[16]

Richard Conway (Ricardo Conveo) was a son of Patrick Conway and his wife whose surname was White. He was born in New Ross, Co. Wexford, in 1572. Before entering the Society of Jesus in Coimbra in 1592 he spent almost two years in the Irish College, Lisbon, from late 1589 until mid-1592, studying an Arts course there. He studied philosophy at the Jesuit College in Monterey and theology at the Royal College, Salamanca. He was ordained in 1600 and joined the staff of the Irish College, Salamanca as confessor and, sometimes, vice-rector.[17] He became rector of the college in 1608 until 1613 when he was transferred as the first Irish Jesuit rector of the Irish College of Santiago de Compostela. During his rectorship there (1613–19) he also acted as procurator[18] of both the Santiago and Salamanca colleges and, in addition, for the Jesuit Mission in Ireland.

15 Op. cit., p. 56.   16 See J. O'Boyle, op. cit., pp 251–5; *Calendar of State Papers, Ireland, 1615–1625* (London, 1860–1912). There is an interesting document, dated 9 March 1613, from the Archives in Simancas which throws light on the differences of opinion about the running of the Santiago college by Fr MacCarthy (ICOL/SANT/1). The ensuing dispute which brought out the deep differences between the O Sullivan Beare and the Gaelic Irish contingent in Spain on one side and on the opposite side the Anglo-Irish priests of the Jesuit order mainly from south Munster who took over the college in 1613 by order of the king. This matter will be treated in greater detail in Chapter 6.   17 There were three vice-rectors in Salamanca in 1592–1605; the other two were Thomas White and James Archer. 18 The office of procurator was an onerous one at the best of times, but Fr Conway was involved in three different areas. The procurator in the Jesuit

After Santiago de Compostela he was moved to Madrid to conduct the financial business of the Irish Colleges in Spain and of the Jesuit Mission in Ireland. Apparently he was successful in financial management. His next assignment, after Madrid, was to take over as the first Jesuit rector of the Seville college in 1619, where he remained for almost three years until recalled once again to Madrid. He returned as rector at Seville in 1625 and died there on 1 December 1626.[19]

The life of Thomas White, the indefatigable founder of many of the Irish Colleges for secular priests in the peninsula, has been well documented. He came from a well-to-do merchant family and was related to the great Franciscan, Fr Luke Wadding (1588–1657) and was connected with the distinguished Munster families of Lombard, Wyse, Walsh and Comerford. He was born in Clonmel c.1556, entered the Society in Villagarcia (the exact date is not known). He travelled extensively and acted as rector for periods in Lisbon, Salamanca and Santiago but he was mostly on the move, seeking support for the colleges. He died in 1622 in Santiago where he was then rector of the Irish College. Over a long and busy life he was greatly supported by Queen Margaret of Spain and many other influential people.[20]

William White, son of John White and Anastatia Comorton, was born in Waterford in 1582 or 1583. He was a cousin of Fr Thomas White. He joined the Irish College in Salamanca in March 1600 and entered the Jesuits in the province of Andalusia in 1605. He studied theology at the Royal College, Salamanca and was ordained there. He acted as confessor to the students in the Irish College, and on occasions conducted retreats outside the college.

organisation was a financial agent or bursar, on the lines of the Roman procurator of an imperial province. **19** Most of the biographical notes on the Jesuit rectors have been taken directly from Fr Francis Finnegan's unpublished 'Biographical Dictionary of Irish Jesuits', already cited (I give these as Finnegan, op. cit. page number) with some additions from other Jesuit records already mentioned in footnote one. Sources outside of these which are mentioned in the course of this chapter will be given in the footnotes. For details of Seville, see also Francis Finnegan SJ, op. cit., *IER*, pp 45–63. **20** See Edmund Hogan SJ, *Distinguished Irishmen of the sixteenth century* (London, 1894), pp 48–70; Fr Finnegan, op. cit., pp 214–15.

He went back to Ireland in 1615 and worked in Waterford until 1622. When his cousin, Fr Thomas White, died, he was sent to Spain to take over as rector in the Irish College at Santiago. If he held the position of rector it may have been only for a short time. He was given leave to return to Ireland because of his poor health but died in Santiago in September 1625.[21]

Thomas Briones (Bryan, Brehon and O'Broin) was born in Kilkenny in 1582, diocese of Ossory.[22] He was son of Thomas Bryan and Joanna Hoyne. He studied at Salamanca in 1600 and entered the Society at Rome on 21 January 1605. After his noviceship he resumed ecclesiastical studies at the Roman College and spent the last year of his course at Ingolstadt in Germany, before returning to Ireland in 1609. For the next four years he was a missionary in Kilkenny. He was called back to Spain and appointed rector in Salamanca in 1613, and he held this office until he became rector of Santiago in 1622 until 1624. He was transferred back to Salamanca as rector in 1626. He then went to Madrid in 1627 as procurator of the Irish mission and the Irish Colleges in the Peninsula until 1631 when he ceased to be a member of the province of Castille and was incardinated in Andalusia. He was immediately appointed rector in Seville from 1631 to 1637. It is reported that the seminarians were very satisfied with him.

For the next four years he was *operarius* at the Residence of Marchena in Andalucía but was re-appointed rector at Seville in response to the demands of the students. He was forced by ill-health and threatened blindness to retire after three years on 1 February 1644 but remained at the college as spiritual father to the seminarians until his death a year later on 12 February 1645.[23]

As Paul Sherlock's autobiography is extant and is in manuscript form in the Russell Library, in NUI Maynooth, I have put an abridged form of it, but still running to several pages, as an addendum at the end of this chapter.

Nicholas White SJ[24] was born in Clonmel in 1598, entered the Irish College in Salamanca and was received into the Society on 15 April 1615 at

21 Fr Finnegan, op. cit., p. 215.   22 Fr Finnegan suggests that his place of birth may have been Jenkinstown, op. cit., p. 19.   23 Finnegan, op. cit., p. 19; Finnegan, op. cit., pp 50–1.   24 Nicholas White appears in some sources as rector around 1628.

Villagarcia. He studied philosophy in Monforte and theology at the Royal College, Salamanca in 1619. He was ordained around the year 1623 and taught humanities in the college at Logroño. In 1625 he was sent to Santiago probably as prefect of studies. He suceeded Fr Sherlock as rector in 1628 and died on 3 October that year at the early age of thirty.

Thadeus O'Sullivan SJ, son of Dermot O Sullivan and Cecilia MacCarthy, was born at Meen, Co. Kerry, around 1596 in the diocese of Ardfert. He studied at the Irish Colleges of Santiago and Salamanca and was ordained in 1622 in Salamanca. On 22 December of that year he was received into the Society in the province of Castille. He was assigned to the Irish College at Santiago, where he became rector in 1629. He returned to Ireland in 1633. He ministered in Kerry but was later stationed at Limerick where he was superior. He was at the Waterford residence during Fr Verdier's visitation to the mission.[25] In his report to the General Fr Verdier praised Fr O Sullivan's 'gifts of character and intellectual ability.'
   In Cromwellian times he was captured, imprisoned by the parliamentarians and transported. He eventually found refuge in Spain in 1655 where he was attached to the Royal College, Salamanca. He was a cousin-germain of Dermicio O Sullivan (son of Donal Cam and Elena O Sullivan Mor), who before his death appointed him executor of his will and also left him a life-annuity. He died at Salamanca on 22 February 1684.[26]

James O'Kearney (Carneo) was son of Philip O Kearney and Helen Sall and was a nephew of Fr Barnaby O'Kearney SJ, another Jesuit, and archbishop David Kearney of Cashel (1603–25). He was born in Cashel in 1601 and entered the Society in Castile on 26 January 1621. He had studied at Santiago and Salamanca where he read two years of philosophy. After his first religious profession he resumed his ecclesiastical studies at the Royal College in Salamanca where he was ordained around 1627. At the end of his studies he was appointed *operarius* at Valladolid where he stayed for three years until he was appointed rector of Santiago in 1631. The superior of the Irish Mission, Fr Robert Nugent, asked that Fr O'Kearney be sent back to work in Ireland but it was decided that he was needed for

25 Fr Mercure Verdier was sent to Ireland as an official visitor by the Jesuit General in Rome. See Michael J. Hynes, *The mission of Rinuccini nuncio extraordinary to Ireland, 1645–1649* (Dublin, 1932), p. 264. 26 Finnegan, op. cit., pp 156–7; *Arch. Hib.* 2 (1913), p. 35; 3 (1914), pp 91–2, fn. 2.

administration in the Irish Colleges. He was rector until 1646 when he was appointed spiritual father at the nearby Jesuit college in Santiago. He died on 9 July 1648. During his career he enjoyed the confidence of the hierarchy as examiner of all candidates for priestly office.[27]

Peter Reid is listed as rector in Santiago in 1647–8 and in Salamanca in 1648–51. He was born in Ratoath, Co. Meath, in 1606, son of Peter Reid and Alison née Beada (Ward or Peart) and ordained in 1633. He published a volume on the *Book of Macchabies* and a planned second volume was not published when he died in 1651.[28]

Ignatius Lombard was born in Waterford in 1614 and entered the Society in Villagarcia in March 1633. After his noviceship he spent a year teaching Humanities at the College of Leon and was then sent for his philosophy course to the college at Santiago. His theology course followed and was at the Royal College, Salamanca from 1639 to 1643, where he was ordained. He was retained at the Royal College to teach Controversial Theology until his appointment as rector of Santiago in 1648. He ruled the college until 1652, when he was sent to Madrid as procurator of the Irish Mission. He remained there for the next fourteen years. He was also the representative of the General at the royal court on business concerning the missions overseas. At times he was entrusted with negotiations between the Holy See and the king of Spain. Fr Finnegan notes that his name is not found in the *Catalogii* of the Toledo province so Lombard is of the opinion that he must have been given special permission to reside outside the Jesuit houses.[29]

Christophero Acuña[30]

William Salinger was born in Kilkenny *c.*1598, diocese of Ossory, and entered the Society in around 1621. He studied philosophy for three years, theology for four and taught *grammatica* for sixteen years. He was a Master and Doctor of Arts. He returned to Ireland and acted as rector in

---

27 Finnegan, op. cit., p. 143. **28** Sal. Arch. XXII/I. *Arch. Hib.* 4 (1915), p. 15; Finnegan, op. cit., p. 164; Catálogos públicos de las provincias de Castilla (Cat. MSS. Hib. SJ, 1556–1669), Jesuit Archives, Dublin, v.i, pp 243–4. **29** Finnegan, op. cit., p. 92. **30** A Spanish rector who was rector for only a short while.

the Jesuit college in Kilkenny before he took up office as rector of the Irish College in Santiago from 1653 to 1660. He died in 1665.[31]

Andrew Lincoln was born in Waterford on 30 November 1622 or 1623 and entered the Society in Castile on 25 June 1642. After his noviceship he spent some time at the college of Pamplona and commenced his ecclesiastical studies at the Royal College, Salamanca and the College of St Ambrose, Valladolid. He was ordained c.1652. He was made rector of the Irish College, Santiago from 1660 until 1666, when he became rector at Salamanca and held this post until his death on 13 February 1686.[32]

Jeremiah Sweetman was born in Meath on 30 September 1634. He entered the Society in Villagarcia in August 1652. After his noviceship he studied philosophy at Santiago and read theology in the Royal College, Salamanca from 1655 to 1659. He was ordained in 1659 and served as minister and taught at Pamplona and Oviedo from 1660 to 1665. He was rector in Santiago from 1666 to 1668. While he was there he conducted parish retreats. He returned to Oviedo as professor of Moral Theology and later held a similar post in the college in Avila. In 1672 he was appointed procurator of the mission and the Irish Colleges in Spain in Madrid until 1682, when he was ordered to leave Spain by royal order. According to Fr Finnegan, it is surmised that it may have had something to do with his success in winning support for the Irish mission and the Irish seminaries in Spain to the detriment of the Spanish Jesuit establishments. The Irish in Spain protested and Fr Sweetman was promised that the Provincial in Portugal would welcome him. However, he died on his way to Portugal at Talavera on 7 October 1683.[33]

Andrew Lynch SJ was son of Luke Lynch and his wife Joan Kirwan and was born in Galway on 30 November 1627. He carried out his ecclesiastical studies at the Irish College, Salamanca where he was ordained. He was received into the Society at Villagarcia on 6 April 1655.

After his noviceship he taught humanities at the College of Santander and then returned to Salamanca in 1658 to complete his theological studies at the Royal College. He was also sent to teach Humanities at the College

---

31 Cat. MSS. Hib. SJ, 1556–1669, pp 356, 379, 415, 417.   **32** Finnegan, op. cit., p. 90.   **33** Ibid., pp 107–8, 415, 434.

of Burgos until he was was appointed rector at Santiago in 1668. He was invited to return to Ireland but the Spanish Superior made representations that he could work just as well for his country at one of the Irish Colleges, as he possessed good talents for government. So he never returned to Ireland but held the rectorship at the Irish College, Santiago up to the time of his death on 1 January 1694.[34]

Barnaby Bathe, son of Andrew Bathe and Mary Sweetman, was born in the diocese of Meath on 10 June 1659. He studied at the Irish College at Santiago and entered the Society in Salamanca in November 1679. He taught at the Jesuit College in La Coruña until 1694. He became rector of the Irish College, Salamanca in 1693 and rector of the Irish College, Santiago from 1695. He died in office on 20 June 1710.[35]

Antonius Cangas

Juan de Mondragon[36]

James (Harrison) O'Connor (Henriques) was son of James O'Connor and Mary Harrison, born in Wexford on 24 September 1679. He carried out his ecclesiastical studies in the Irish College, Salamanca and entered the Society in Villagarcia on 10 January 1703. He used his mother's name Harrison, or its Spanish equivalent Henriques, in the records. He was made rector of the Irish College, Santiago in 1712 and died in office on 4 January 1724.[37]

John Harrison (Henriques) was a brother of another James Harrison (1695–1769) who was also a Jesuit (not the previous rector). He was born in Kilmuckridge, near Enniscorthy, Co. Wexford, on 28 July 1682, son of Peter Harrison and Joan Grace. He entered the Society on 29 November 1702. He studied philosophy for a year at the Irish College, Santiago. After his first religious profession he was sent back there to complete his course of philosophy. He was ordained before 1711. He taught philosophy in Valladolid in 1714 until 1724. In his last year he was professor of Dogmatic

---

34 Finnegan, op. cit., p. 95.   **35** Ibid., p. 7.   **36** Two Spanish rectors who acted for relatively short periods.   **37** Finnegan, op. cit., p. 135. The reason for using Henriques or Harrison here is difficult to explain. The use of Spanish equivalents of surnames was probably for convenience. Sal. Arch. 34/7, 39/12.

Theology. In 1724 he was appointed rector in Santiago de Compostela until the rectorship of Salamanca fell vacant in October 1728. Fr Finnegan tells us that 'he was not long in office [in Salamanca] when his administration at Compostela came in for severe criticism on the part of the Spanish superiors. According to these Harrison left the college burdened with debts while discipline was relaxed duing his period of office.' He seems to have had difficult times as rector in both colleges. Things reached a crisis when he arrived back in Ireland in 1732. His career is somewhat chequered until he finally returned to Spain where he was assigned by the General to the province of Aragon in 1735. He was an operarius in Osca until his death on 20 February 1738.

Fr Finnegan tells us that John Harrison was undoubtledly a man of zeal and intellectual ability 'but events proved that he lacked all aptitude for administration and understood nothing of the diplomatic ways of settling difficulties. His break with the Castile province was deplorable not only for his own sake but for its consequences affecting the Irish Jesuit mission. That province for a century and a half had proved itself the missions best friend amongst all the provinces of the Society, considering the number of young Irish men it had trained for service in Ireland. The bitterness and suspicion aroused by Harrison was the reason that for ten years no Irishman would be received in Castile for the Society.'[38]

The last two Jesuit rectors of the college were Spanish. When the Society was suppressed in 1767 the archbishop of Santiago, don Bartolemé Rajoy, appointed a secular priest as acting-superior of the Irish College. This was an unfortunate appointment for several reasons. Fr Pedro Rodríguez was parish priest of the Church of Sta. Maria Salomé, which was, of course, opposite the Irish College in the Rua Nueva. The students objected, not on that account but because he commenced to maintain his nephews and their teachers in the college at the college's expense.[39] The students obviously had friends in high places. The important general and minister of King Carlos III, don Pedro Pablo Abarca de Bolea, conde de Aranda (1719–1798), intervened in the matter.[40] He asked the archbishop to

---

38 Fr Finnegan, op. cit., pp 72–3.   39 Couselo, op. cit., p. 17.   40 Aranda, as he is usually called, was a minister of state, a general, a diplomat and belonged to an ancient, noble Aragonese family. He was responsible for the expulsion and suppression of the Jesuits whom the king blamed for the riots in Madrid in 1766. He had been exiled to his estates by Fernando VI but was recalled by Charles III

remove Fr Rodriguez 'por no ser sujeto de las circunstancias y literatura necesaria para el gobierno, dirección y enseñanza de los nobles irlandeses, que por ser su profesión y destino se han de emplear en asunto tan útil e importante, como es la predicación y conversión de los herejes a nuestra religión; y por otra parte ademaá de tener el expresado D. Pedro tan pocas condiciones para el gobierno, tratando a los seminaristas con poco respeto y consideración, mantenía a costa del colegio a sus sobrinos y profesores que les enseñaban' (because he is not an individual with the qualifications or letters necessary for the governance, direction and teaching of the Irish nobles who by their profession and destiny have to be employed in a matter so useful and important, as is preaching to and converting the heretics to our religion; and in addition apart from the said D. Pedro having so few requisites for ruling [the students], treating the seminarians with little respect, he was maintaining at the expense of the college his nephews and the teachers who taught them).[41]

The appointment of the parish priest was also unwise as the relations between the college and the parish priests of that church had not always been happy ones. There were instances of disputes from time to time with the local *parroco*, for example, about fees payable on the death of students in the college and fees for Easter duties. One example took place in April 1682 when a student died of smallpox and the rector had to pay the parish priest 36 *reales* for the funeral expenses. This charge was to cover the vigil, funeral and mass and for the sacristan who rang the bell, carried the cross and offered prayers. The archbishop of Santiago in response to Aranda's intervention instructed his *provisor* (bursar) to dismiss the priest and to investigate the matter and to appoint one of the two priests suggested by the Irish.[42] Couselo cites a letter signed by Frs Nicolas Mullen, Philip Hassett, Walter Moloney, James Devine and clerical students, Walter Blake and Edmund Quinn, who had no objection to the priest as acting-superior provided his nephews and their teacher left the college. Fr Patrick Kenney, who was confessor with languages in the cathedral of Santiago, was appointed as acting-superior.[43]

on his sucession to the throne. He was made President of the Council of State and Captain-general of New Castile and was the most powerful minister in Spain. Later, in 1792 he was prime minister for a short time under Carlos IV. **41** Couselo, op. cit., p. 17.   **42** Ibid.; Sal. Arch. XXIV/I, 35/1, 34/8.   **43** I have not found any further details of Fr Kenney. Couselo, op. cit., pp 17, 18.

ADDENDUM: AUTOBIOGRPHY OF PAUL SHERLOCK SJ

In 1917 Dr Amalio Huarte published[44] a memorial found in the Archives of the University of Salamanca, taken from an *expediente* (a file of papers) which was an autobiography written in his own hand by Fr Paul Sherlock SJ, former rector of the Irish Colleges of Santiago de Compostela and Salamanca. Huarte suggested that this account of his life must have been written by Sherlock in order to give proof that his library had been purchased from his own funds and not from those of the Irish College as was subsequently claimed after his death, when the Colegio Real of the Society of Jesus in Santiago asserted that the library belonged to that college and requested its transfer to that institution. The matter was debated at an inquiry held by the acting-chancellor (*maestrescuela*) of the University. It was finally resolved in favour of the Colegio Real. Four students from the Irish College, Salamanca defended the view that it should be retained by the Irish College. They were Bernard Reilly, William Dardis, Peter Daly and Patrick White.[45]

Whatever the reason for the composition of the autobiography the memorial, now held in the NUI Maynooth, Russell Library, is an invaluable source. It contains much information not only on the life of the eminent Jesuit scholar, Paul Sherlock, but on both the Irish colleges of Salamanca and Santiago.

Paul Sherlock was born in Waterford city on 14 August 1595. He was a son of Walter Sherlock and Beatrice Leonard. He had at least two brothers, Patrick and John. He received a Catholic education and claimed reasonable Latin when he left Ireland at 16 years of age. He landed in Bilbao on 10 May 1612, arriving in Salamanca early in July. He entered the

---

44 The article 'El P. Paulo Sherlock: una autobiografía inédita' appeared in *Arch. Hib.* 6 (1917), pp 156–72, with a synopsis in English by Mrs Helen Concannon, pp 171–4.   45 Ibid., p. 156 and fn.3 same page. William Dardis, diocese of Meath, was a student at the Irish College of Santiago de Compostela in 1644 before continuing on to Salamanca where he took the oath on 11 February 1646. Peter Daly, diocese of Clonfert, had also been a student in Santiago before going on to Salamanca. The other two, Bernard Reilly, diocese of Ardagh and Patrick White, diocese of Waterford, were students at Salamanca in the 1640s and probably had studied philosophy at Santiago prior to that. I have not found records of their stay in Santiago: *Arch. Hib.* 6 (1917), p. 156. It also appears (Sal. Arch. 33/1/14) that Fr Sherlock sought and obtained permisssion of the General in 1637 to donate his library to the Jesuit residence in Waterford.

Society of Jesus (after three months in the seminary) in the Colegio Real, Salamanca on 30 September 1612, together with his fellow Waterfordman, Thomas White, and was received into the order by Fr Gaspar de Vega, the provincial. He spent most of his novitiate in Villagarcia and Medina del Campo. At the end of two years he was sent to Santiago de Compostela to study Arts under his brother, Patrick, who was a teacher in the Irish College there, having been received into the Society on 10 April 1602 but who died in Santiago on 18 August 1614, two months before Paul's arrival there. His brother, John, aged 18 years, was in the Irish College, Salamanca from 24 April 1604.[46]

He was sent to St Ambrose's in Valladolid to continue his studies. When he finished his arts course he continued theology in that college for the first and second year courses. He then returned to Santiago for the third and fourth years. He was ordained in 1621 and celebrated his first mass on the feast of the Most Holy Trinity. More studies followed in St Ambrose's and the College of Monterey. In 1624 he was to take a post-graduate course in Pamplona, but he fell ill and spent his convalescence in the college of Bellimar. Soon afterwards, on his recovery, he conducted a mission there which gave him and his listeners great spiritual satisfaction.

Paul Sherlock was ordered to take over the rectorship of the Irish College at Santiago de Compostela in 1624. The taking over of such a task was, he says, 'de increíble molestía'.[47] Around this time he made up his mind to start writing a commentary on the Canticle of Canticles (the Song of Songs), *Cantares de Salomón*. The studies he carried out for this had to be done at night and he continued at them in Santiago and also some time after he went as rector to Salamanca.[48]

The cold he suffered during these nights of study were a particular cross to bear and this and his self-inflicted hardships remind one of Francisco de Quevedo y Villegas (1580–1605), the great Spanish satirist and poet, a nobleman, a diplomat and Knight of Santiago, who spent four years in prison for a satire on the powerful *válido* (favourite), the Duque de Olivares. Like Sherlock he suffered habitually from the cold. In the final scene from Alejandro Casona's moving drama, *El caballero de las espuelas*

---

46 *Arch. Hib.* 2 (1913), p. 17.   **47** Translation: 'of unbelievable hardship' for him. Apparently, the appointments as rector were burdens to him and he undertook them only in obedience and as the will of God.   **48** Fray Luís de León (1528–1591), University of Salamanca, was the great interpreter of the Book of Job and the Canticle of Canticles.

de oro (The knight of the golden spurs), on the life of the sixteenth-century satirist, the dying Quevedo pleads with the Lord:

> Lord, You have given me a long life of punishment and I have obeyed without question. At first I believed that my punishment was the cold. Then I believed it was solitude. It has taken me a whole lifetime to understand that solitude and cold are one and the same thing. If I were to be born again and You were to condemn me to being alone, I would obey You. But alone for eternity, no. Don't leave me outside with my solitude and my cold … Open Your door, Oh Lord, open for me.[49]

Fr Sherlock was rector in the Galician college until the end of 1629[50] when he was appointed rector in the Irish College, Salamanca. He continued his research on the Canticles in Salamanca and continued to work late into the night. He states that around this time he commenced *a poner en limpio* (the final version or fair copy of) the first volume which appeared in Lyon in 1633, printed by the Cardon brothers.[51] Sherlock speaks also of a vision which he had in 1629, of St Brendan the Navigator, the sixth-century Irish abbot. In it the saint anointed the fingers of his right hand as if encouraging him in the important work he was carrying out. He was apparently also given to practising severe mortifications and stringent punishments which were not included in the prescribed devotions of his order. His failing health forced him to terminate the more extreme practices.[52] He had also great devotion to the Virgin Mary and he says he had felt her palpable protection and help and had on occasions visions of her.

49 Alejandro Casona, *El caballero de las espuelas de oro* (Madrid, 1965, Colección Austral), pp 93–4.   50 He tells us that he became rector of the Salamanca college in 1628 but Huarte (op. cit., p. 161, fn.1) points out that Fr Thomas Briones presented the last accounts of his period of office as rector in Salamanca on 30 April 1629 and Sherlock did not take up office until May of that year.   51 The city of Lyon was at that time one of the principal and most important centres of printing, and the Cardon family specialised in publishing for the Society of Jesus. The other printer of Sherlock's work was Prost, also one of the foremost printers in Lyon. See Penelope Woods, 'Books rich, rare and curious' in Agnes Neligan (ed.), *Maynooth Library treasures* (Dublin, 1995), pp 29–63, 42–3 and S. Legay, 'Les fréres Cardon, marchands-libraires à Lyon, 1600–35', *Bulletin du Bibliophile* (1991), pp 416–20.   52 An example was the hair shirt.

As rector he found the college finances in a bad way – grants had not been paid for years – and in Salamanca he was forced to cut back the intake of students entering the seminary. He decided that he must do something about the situation and went forthwith to Madrid, to the court, to plead for funds. He was again very unhappy but finally succeeded in ways he never imagined; his requests for funds were successful and the situation was regulated for both the Santiago and Salamanca colleges. This was surprising, since the funds of the Irish Colleges were often taken from the war chest and it was a time of heavy expenditure on some fronts. He was assisted by Queen Margarita, the Austrian wife of Philip IV, who in her will left a legacy to the college in Salamanca. He was able to do several repairs in 1638, and in 1639 he rebuilt the refectory which had collapsed. In the same year the Provincial of the Jesuits appointed him to the chair of Scripture in the Colegio Real of the Society in Salamanca.

In 1640 all three volumes of the commentary on the Canticles were printed in Lyon by Jacobo Prost, with an expanded single volume, and from sales earned 20,000 *reales vellón*. The bishop of Cuzco, to whom he dedicated the work, gave him 8,000 *reales de plata* which, at that time, was double the value of the *real de vellón*, in other words 16,000 *reales*. Significantly, he states that with the money he spent 26,000 *reales* on the library which he had in the seminary, so that this library, he states, belongs totally to the Jesuit Order, because not a penny of the cost came from the seminary funds. In 1640 also he commenced the tract, *Scientia Media* and the bishop of Puebla de los Angeles in New Spain (Mexico), Juan de Palafox de Menda, the same year undertook to give 100 ducats each year to the seminary in Salamanca.[53]

In 1641 the bishop of Dertonese, Italy, Paulo Aresio, a Theatine, published a pamphlet attacking the first volume of the Canticles and a new edition of it appeared in Venice. The following year the Marqués de Taragona made available to the Irish College an annual sum of 120 ducats.

---

53 Bishop Palafox was appointed bishop of Angelopolis (Puebla de los Ángeles) in Mexico in 1539. He was a saintly man who made strenuous efforts to protect the native people from oppression. He made powerful enemies and was eventually transferred to the see of Osma, a small diocese, in old Castile in 1653. He was beatified in 1694. See *Encyclopaedia Britannica,* vols 19–20, p. 593. Dr Downey is of the opinion that these two bishops may have been professors in Santiago or Salamanca in their earlier careers, and he recalls seeing portraits of them in the cloister of the Rectorate of the University of Santiago de Compostela.

In 1643 Sherlock was made Qualificator of the Holy Office in the Tribunal of Valladolid. *De Scientia Media* was published in Lyon in 1644 with the author's name given as Paul Leonard (his mother's maiden name) and without the SJ. His health was very bad at this time and he resigned the chair of Scripture in the Colegio Real and his physical condition continued to deteriorate until his death in August 1646.

He was a man of exemplary character and deep holiness. He was criticised at the time for his inadequate handling of the college finances, and the accusation was made that he used college funds to augment the college library which he had at his disposition, and it was said that he had made bad investments of the college money in *juros* and *censos* which did not yield dividends and had to be sold later at great loss. Huarte indicates that the Superior of the Society of Jesus had the finances of the college reviewed at a later stage.[54] It must be said, however, that it appears that he did succeed in bringing in various financial contributions to the college through his efforts at fund-raising.

54 Op. cit., p. 163.

CHAPTER 5

The Students

The list of students of the Irish College, Santiago de Compostela which follows, together with the special biographical notes on each, is compiled from several main sources. These sources vary, and the data about the collegians is by its nature limited. Sometimes it consists merely of a name and a date – for example, when a student swore an oath to adhere to the rules of his college and promised to return to 'the Mission', as Ireland was termed at that time. In fact, the starting point for most of the potted biographies of each collegian is the oath or oaths sworn at different times during the student's career.

The principal manuscript source is the Salamanca Archives, a major collection of manuscripts relating to the Irish continental colleges in Spain which is housed in the Russell Library, NUI Maynoth.[1]

Information about the early students of the Irish College of Santiago de Compostela (foundation date 1605) is almost non-existent. What is available is fragmentary, meagre and has been gleaned from three sources:

1. The report of Patrick Sinnott, Master of Arts, University of Santiago (*Información de Patricio Cisnote, Maestro de Gramática en la Universidad de Santiago acerca del Sem.o Irlandés de la dicha ciudad de Santiago*) on the Irish seminary of the city of Santiago. The date of this report or memorial is 28 December 1612. Sinnott reports that there were twelve students at the start of the college and since that date some have left, others have come in their place, only two have become priests, and the rest have gone to war or followed other careers. He recalls the names of only ten students, five of whom he mentions by name, and five obliquely without exact or complete

---

1 The material relating to the Irish College at Santiago de Compostela is to be found mainly in *legajos* (files or dossiers) numbered XXIII/I/i and ii, XXII/2, XXIV/I, 33/I/1–15, 34/2, 34/4, 34/7, 34/8, 35/4 and others. The abbreviation used for this source in this chapter and elsewhere in this work is 'Sal. Arch. and dossier number'. Another important manuscript source is the Jesuit Archive, Leeson Street, Dublin.

names. These are Thomas Geraldino (FitzGerald); Cornelio Driscol; Florencio (Mac) Carthy; another with surname Ussi (Hussey) and his brother; another with surnamed Molina; another 'of the Driscoles', his brother Thadeo, a cousin and a brother of the latter.[2]

2. The declarations of the students at the time of the takeover of the college by the Jesuits in 1613, mostly dated 24 April 1613, and made before D. Diego de la Hoz, *provisor* (vicar general) of the archdiocese of Santiago. D. Pedro Maldonado, rector of the college of the Society of Jesus of Santiago de Compostela[3] had issued instructions that, to fulfil His Majesty's orders, statements should be taken from each student, indicating his wishes with regard to acceding to the king's orders to subject himself to the government and conditions which pertain in all the other seminaries of Irish and English in the kingdom of Spain and which are in the charge of the Society of Jesus. The students are: Philip Holland (O'Houleghan, O'Houlihan), Denis Driscoll, Florence Carty, Buecio (Boethius) O Sullivan (students of Jurisprudence), Daniel O Sullivan, Charles Carthy, *maestro* Philip O Sullivan (the author), Dermetro Driscoll, Edward Suitman (Sweetman), Cornelio O Driscoll and Richard Sinnott. There are eleven names and nine declarations.[4]

3. Domhnall O Sullivan Beare's list, undated but probably *c.*1617, which is included in his memorial against the takeover of the college by the Jesuits. In this he gives nine names and states that 'although there is no obligation to become priests, they themselves by their own desire do so and thus out of it have come Fr Cornelius O'Driscol, Benedictine monk, Fr Eugeneo Field, Franciscan, both qualified in Theology and Preachers, Fr Daniel Hanglio (Anglim), Franciscan, also about to be ordained, Don Felipe O Sullivan (Philip O'Sullivan Beare), nephew of the Lord of Birhaven (O Sullivan Beare himself), Master of Arts and Bachelor of Canon Law; the remainder are students of Arts, Philosophy and Canon Law, some graduated and others about to be; also (from this house) Bachelors Molina Cantio, and Raymundo Hussey, the last-named Jurist and the former Theologian, and as

---

2 This list is to be found in Sal. Arch. 35/4; some details of Patrick Sinnott will be found in Chapter 6. The name Molina could possibly be Mullen. Elsewhere this individual is described as Molina Canty (Carty?). See Patricia O Connell, 'The Irish College, Santiago de Compostela, 1605–1767', *Arch. Hib.* (1996), pp 19–28. **3** In the document he claims to be also rector of the Irish seminary.   **4** Sal. Arch. 33/1/15, 35/4. The Jesuits took over on Friday 26 April 1613 and the students were dismissed on 29 Monday.

well Don Tadeo O Drischol, eldest son of Don Dermisio (O Drischol) with three years of Arts and two of Canon Law, son of the lord of Castlehaven, Don Daniel O'Drischol, son of the Lord of Baltimor, to whom, his Arts studies finished, His Majesty favoured with a grant for Flanders, and Don Thomas Geraldino, heir to the *Señor del Vale* (Knight of Glin), also favoured by His Majesty with a grant for Flanders.'[5]

The main printed sources include María-José Arnáiz & José-Luis Sancho, *El colegio de los irlandeses* (Alcalá de Henares, 1985); this work gives a list of the students sent, in 1649, from Santiago de Compostela to the recently founded Irish College in Alcalá de Henares; a series of articles by the Revd Denis O'Doherty in *Archivium Hibernicum*, 'Students of the Irish College Salamanca (1595–1617), v.2 (1913), pp 1–36; (1619–1700), v.3 (1914) pp 87–112; (1715–1778), v.4 (1915), pp 1–58 (this monumental work offers details of Salamanca students, many of whom went from Santiago to Salamanca after their initial studies in philosophy in the Galician college); José Couselo Bouzas, *El colegio de irlandeses de Santiago de Compostela* (Santiago, 1935); this work includes names of 54 students 25 of whom were not found in other sources during the period; E. Rivera Vázquez, *Galicia y los jesuitas: sus colegios y enseñanza en los siglos XVI al XVIII* (Santiago, 1989) with much useful information on the college and collegians.[6]

As the list of students, with their biographical details, is long, I have tried to restrict the number of footnotes. For each name I have, therefore, given one footnote and within this have included in many cases a number of references or sources relating to the main facts about the student. The bulk of the references are to the MSS or printed works just cited.[7]

The rules of the Irish Colleges were strict and closely adhered to. One rule was that each student swore an oath, or *juramento*, making various promises. The oath was written down by the collegian in his own handwriting, dated and finally signed by him and generally witnessed by two of his fellow students. It was then sealed with the college seal. Dr

5 Sal. Arch. 33/1/15 (translations by Patricia O Connell).   **6** Other titles are given in the Bibliography.   **7** The abbreviated forms for the printed works are respectively Arnáiz-Sancho plus page number; *Arch. Hib.* vols 2, 3 or 4 and page number(s). I have to pay special tribute to Dr O'Doherty who in the early 1900s gathered together this rich source into three articles in *Arch. Hib.* with copious and scholarly notes added; Couselo plus page number; Rivera plus page number.

Denis O'Doherty tells us that on the seal 'in the early days in Salamanca there was a figure of St Patrick, the Patron and Titular, with mitre and crozier, surmounted by an archiepiscopal cross, the right hand extended in blessing, with a serpent at his feet.'[8]

The *juramentos* had standard forms, the most usual being the triple oath. In very simple terms this was to observe the college rules and strive for perfection, to take Holy Orders and return to service on the mission. Dr O'Doherty gives the various forms in his series of article referred to above.[9] Those who entered religious orders were exempted from fulfilling the oath to return to Ireland. There was also another oath by which the students bonded themselves to say five masses per week for the rector's intentions and two masses as often as he gave them a stipend.

The students studied philosophy in the Irish College, Santiago de Compostela, for two years. They then went on to the Irish College, Salamanca for three years theology (Moral and Dogmatic). This course entailed examinations for first, second and third year theology, usually in July or August. Some of the students also defended *Dominicales, Controversias* or *Conclusiones*, all various forms of theological debates generally held in the Royal College, which was the headquarters of the Jesuit Order in Santiago. Very often the students were ordained in minor orders in Santiago *de prima y menores, de prima y grados, de tonsura y menores, de corona y grados*.[10] Some were ordained to the priesthood, i.e., *de misa* or *de presbítero*, in Santiago also.

ACKET *see* HACKETT

EDWARD ALERVERT was sent to the newly-opened Irish College in Alcalá de Henares from the Irish College, Santiago de Compostela in 1649.[11]

---

8 In Salamanca the inscription was *Sigillum Seminarii Hibernorum Salaman.* In Santiago it was *Collegii Hibernorum Compostellanorum.* **9** See notes on the various forms in *Arch. Hib.* 2, pp 1–7; 4, pp 1–12. In Santiago the oath was usually taken on St Patrick's Day, in Salamanca on a variety of dates. The rule to return to Ireland was strict. If the student found he had not a vocation and left he was free to go but it was customary for him to repay monies spent on him for the period he was in the college, at the rate of 60 ducats a year. **10** See *Catholic Encyclopedia* on CD-ROM for details of minor orders. **11** Arnáiz-Sancho, pp 61, 87–8. Nine students and Fr Godfrey Daniel were sent to the Irish College, Alcalá de Henares when it was set up in 1649. The college had been planned for several years by a Portuguese nobleman, don Jorge de Paz de Silveira, who died before its

PATRICK ALLEN was sent to the Irish College, Salamanca in 1697 from Santiago, where he had been examined in the whole Arts course. He was examined in first year theology on 1 October 1698 and entered second year theology. Could he be Patrick Allen who was appointed parish priest in 1727 of the parish of Ratoath, Co. Meath?[12]

MATHEW ARCHBOLD was in the college in 1657 and paid 200 *reales* when he entered. He was presented for minor orders in Santiago de Compostela on 16 September 1660 by the rector, William Salinger. He appears in the examination list in Salamanca on 6 October 1663 and was approved by the examiners.[13]

MICHAEL BARON paid 500 *reales* in Santiago in 1623.[14]

REGINAL BARRY (de Barro), student in the Irish College, Santiago, paid 200 *reales* in 1623.[15]

THOMAS BARRY (Barrio) entered the college in Santiago in 1657 and paid 100 *reales*.[16]

BARNABY BATHE SJ arrived in Salamanca in October 1679 from Santiago where he had been examined previously and approved. He was later rector in Salamanca from 1693 until transferred to the Irish College, Santiago as rector in 1695. He died in office. A son of Andrew Bathe and Mary Sweetman, he was born on 10 June 1659 in Athcarne, Co. Meath.[17]

MICHAEL BATHE took the oath in Santiago on 17 March 1710.[18]

foundation. See also Patricia O Connell, *The Irish College at Alcalá de Henares, 1649–1785* (Dublin, 1997). The nine students were Eduardo Alervet, Diego Bruno, Diego Comerfort, Francisco Delamor, Daniel Falon, Domingo Fayon, Angelo Golden, Tomás O'Sullivan, Hugo Porcel.   **12** It was customary for students to study philosophy for two years (initially it was for three years) in Santiago and then transfer to Salamanca to complete their three year course in theology. See Denis O'Doherty, 'Students of the Irish College, Salamanca', *Arch. Hib.* 4, p. 22; 'Index to the priests of the Meath diocese 1707–1993' by Rev. P. Connell in Olive Curran (ed.), *History of the diocese of Meath, 1860–1993* (Mullingar, 1995), p. 1224. Hereinafter the shortened forms will be used, the form for the last named title will be *Meath Index*, plus page number.   **13** Sal. Arch. XXIII/2, 34/2. f. 57v; *Arch. Hib.* 4, p. 17. Maybe a member of a Cork merchant family?   **14** Sal. Arch. S 34/2, f. 17.   **15** Ibid.   **16** Ibid. f. 57v.   **17** *Arch. Hib.* 4, p. 20; Finnegan, op. cit., p. 7.   **18** Sal. Arch. XXIII/I/ii.

FRANCIS BERMINGHAM took the oath in Santiago on 17 March 1743. He was from Dalgan in the Tuam diocese. He went on to Salamanca, arrived there in July 1745 and took the oath on 1 August 1745. He was examined on 16 July 1746 at the end of his first year which he 'answered middlingly', according to the rector, John O'Brien. He returned to Ireland suddenly and mysteriously on 3 February 1747, 'not wishing to follow his studies nor his vocation of missionary: he refused to state the cause'. He died in Jamaica in 1749 where his father sent him, not wishing 'to keep him in his house, in Dalgan'. We are told that his name was so odious to the students in Salamanca that the name in the records of another student named Bermingham was changed to Nugent. This was to cause the latter problems at a later stage when the latter needed his records on his appointment as professor of Greek in the University of Coimbra[19]

PATRICK BERMINGHAM went from Santiago to Salamanca in 1697 and passed his first year examination there on 1 October 1698[20]

ROBERT BETHAL, who also appears as Bethet, came to Salamanca from Santiago on 22 April 1758. He left for Ireland with six other newly ordained priests in June 1760. He was parish priest of Lusk, Co. Dublin, until 1762, Swords 1762 until 1766, then Rathfarnham. He died 1791 as parish priest of St Audeon's and vicar-general of Dublin.[21]

ANTHONY BLAKE took the oath in Santiago on 17 March 1722 and in Salamanca on 6 July 1724. He received minor orders (*prima y menores*) on 21 March 1724 in Santiago. He passed his second year examination on 26 September 1725 and his last year of theology on 27 September 1726. He left for Ireland on 28 July 1727 or 1728.[22]

---

19 Sal. Arch. XXIII/I/ii, 34/7; *Arch. Hib.* 4, pp 7, 31, 32; see also *Sal. Letters,* p. 9 (Sal. Arch. XIII/75), letter 13 AA I, 75, dated 2 March 1747, written from Lisbon to rector John O'Brien, Salamanca. *The Salamanca Letters* is made up of three sections (a) a chronological list of letters in English from the Salamanca Archives, *legajo XIII,* 1625–1871, (b) an alphabetical list of letters in Spanish from the same source, 1625–1871 and (c) the collected letters of each writer in section (b), have been brought together in folders. The folders have then been listed alphabetically under the names of the writers whose letters are contained in each folder. **20** *Arch. Hib.* 4, p. 22. **21** *Arch. Hib.* 4, p. 40; Sal. Arch. I/3; N. Donnelly, *A short history of some Dublin parishes,* part XV (*c.*1915), pp 76, 109. **22** Sal. Arch. XIII/I/ii; *Arch. Hib.* 4, pp 5, 26.

EDWARD BLAKE was in the Santiago college in 1735 and had an account in the college ledger.[23]

JAMES BLAKE was in the college in 1746 and took the oath on St Patrick's Day. He arrived in Salamanca in December 1748. He took the oath there on 17 March 1749 and entered the Franciscan Order in June of that year. Having a great reputation for holiness he had received minor orders in Santiago from Bishop Gil Taboada on 14 November 1747, as he was too young for ordination to the priesthood. In December 1748, as he had reached the required age, he was, in fact, ordained a priest in Avila by the bishop of the diocese. However, shortly afterwards he died in the novitiate.[24]

PATRICK BLAKE entered Santiago on 27 October 1739 and took the oath there on 17 March 1740. In Salamanca on 29 August 1743 he was examined and approved in his first year theology. On 28 July 1744 he and his fellow students did not give satisfaction in their examination 'because they applied themselves more to moral than to dogmatic theology'. However, in his second year he was ordained in March 1745 and had left for Ireland by 25 June 1745. He had been presented for minor orders in Santiago by rector Didacus Araujo according to an undated document.[25]

WALTER (ANTHONY) BLAKE took the oath on 18 March 1767 in Santiago and after his two years of philosophy there went to Salamanca, arriving on 25 June 1768, to study theology and philosophy. He gave signs of application at examination 6 September 1768. He is mentioned as Walter Anthony Black in a list of theology students being kept within the college for the whole year 1769–70 by order of the rector, Peter Sinnott, and forbidden to attend the university. Blake was ordained in minor orders (*tonsura y menores*) on 21 September 1770 and on 21 December 1771 as deacon. He was elected vice-president of the Irish College, Salamanca on 12 September 1772 and on 20 September ordained a priest by Bishop Felipe Beltrán.[26]

23 Sal. Arch. 34/7. Document 34/7 is a ledger containing, among other data, personal accounts of the students with the college. **24** Sal. Arch. XXIII/I/ii; *Arch. Hib.* 4, pp 8, 33, 34; Couselo, op. cit., p. 24. **25** He had his belonging taken from him in San Sebastian and needed clothes, which cost 262 *reales*. Sal. Arch. I/3, XXIII/I/ii, XXIII/2, 34/7; *Arch. Hib.* 4, pp 29, 30, 31. **26** Sal. Arch. XXIII/I/ii, 52/5/14; *Arch. Hib.* 4, pp 46, 48, 49, 50. Sinnott, a secular priest, was rector in Salamanca in 1769–73. On 19 August 1772 he was deposed because of his 'mismanagement'. On 23 October 1769 by order of the Consejo the students and effects were transferred from St Patrick's college to the south wing of the Jesuit

GREGORY BODKIN was in the Santiago college in 1660 and paid 55 *reales* towards his outfit.[27]

JOHN BODKIN came to Salamanca from Santiago in October 1673. He left the seminary in Salamanca in 1675 because of ill health.[28]

LAWRENCE BOYLE was ordained in minor orders on 17 March 1729 by the archbishop of Santiago, don José de Yermo y Santibáñez.[29]

DENIS BRADY took the oath in Santiago on 17 March 1737, proceeded to Salamanca, swore the oath there on 12 September 1739, and passed second theology on 22 August 1740. According to a letter dated 22 January 1755 to the rector of Salamanca from Patrick Masterson he was from the diocese of Kilmore.[30]

WILLIAM BRETT took the oath in Santiago on 17 March 1727[31] and received minor orders (*tonsura menores*) on 17 March 1729 in Santiago from Archbishop Yerma y Santibáñez. In 1730 he was examined in Salamanca and approved for second year theology with a high encomium[32]

BRIEN *see* O'BRIEN

BRITT *see* BRETT

ANTHONY BRODER(S) took the oath in Santiago on 17 March 1764, 24 March 1765 and 17 March 1766, arrived in Salamanca on 11 June 1766 and on 18 June took the oath there. In 1766 he suffered from a wasting disease and on 15 July received Holy Viaticum from the rector. He survived and was ordained on 13 June 1767.[33]

JOHN BRODIR was a student in Santiago in 1613 and paid 510 *reales* for some clothes supplied to him and to Edward Hore in the college.[34]

BRODY *see* BROHY

JAMES BROHY was in Santiago in 1667 and is listed as James Brody. He paid a *limosna* (alms) of 320 *reales*. He went to Salamanca from Santiago in October 1670. He was examined and approved for second year theology

college: see *Arch. Hib.* 4 (1915), pp 46–7. Santiago was closed in 1769.   **27** Sal. Arch. S 34/2, f. 63.   **28** *Arch. Hib.* 4, p. 19.   **29** Couselo, op. cit., p. 24.   **30** Sal. Arch. XXIII/I/ii, 52/5/9; *Arch. Hib.* 4, pp 7, 29.   **31** The MSS. XXIII/I/ii, cites 1720 which has to be an error.   **32** Sal. Arch. XXIII/I/ii; Couselo, op. cit., p. 24; *Arch. Hib.* 4, p. 27.   **33** Sal. Arch. XXIII/I/ii; *Arch. Hib.* 4, pp 11, 45.   **34** Sal. Arch. 34/2, f. 5.

in Salamanca on 13 October 1671 and for third year on 2 October 1672. He was parish priest of St Catherine's, Meath Street, Dublin, 1689–1711, and was ordained in Segovia. He died in 1711.[35]

IGNATIUS BROWNE SJ was in the college in 1649 and was presented by the rector, Ignatius Lombard, for minor orders in Santiago on 16 December 1650. He and two brothers, Peter and Ignatius Saul, paid the sum of 800 *reales* to the college in 1649. He could be Ignatius Brown SJ, born Waterford 1 November 1630, who entered the Society 27 June 1651, lived in Drogheda and Dublin, went eventually to Poitiers 1674 and died in Valladolid in 1679.[36]

JAMES BROWN was one of the Santiago students sent to the Irish College in Alcalá de Henares in 1649 at its foundation. The rector of Santiago states that Fr Wadding SJ sent him 2,000 *reales* for the maintenance of five of the students sent to Alcalá. Could he be James Brown SJ, born Dublin 26 September 1630, who studied philosophy at Santiago, was ordained 1658/9 and died 1686?[37]

THOMAS BROWN was in Santiago in 1667 and paid *limosnas* of 224 *reales* and 600 *reales* to the college. He went to Salamanca in October 1670 where he was examined and approved. He signed the oath there in 1671. On 13 October 1671 and 2 October 1672 he was examined for second and third year theology respectively.[38]

DE BURGO *see* BURKE

JEREMIAH BURKE was in the Santiago college in 1617.

JOHN BURKE entered the college in Santiago on 26 December 1638. He came with two other students Richard Burke and Andrew Kieron and they made a payment of 1,000 *reales*. There is also mention of a barrel of salmon and another of *manteca* (butter or lard) worth 250 *reales*.[40]

MATHEW BURKE (Borque) was in the college in 1670 and paid 100 *reales*.[41]

---

35 *Arch. Hib.* 4, p. 18; Sal. Arch. 34/2, f. 72; N. Donnelly, op. cit., part XIX, pp 215, 217. **36** Sal. Arch. XXIII/2, 34/2, f. 41; Finnegan, op. cit., p. 17. **37** Arnáiz-Sancho, pp 61, 87–88; Sal. Arch. 34/2, f. 41. **38** *Arch. Hib.* 3, p. 108; v.4, p. 18; Sal. Arch. 33/1/14, 34/2, ff. 72, 80 – this last folio may relate to a second Thomas Brown as the *limosna* is later. **39** Sal. Arch. 34/2, f. 10 v. **40** Sal. Arch. S 34/2, f. 34v. **41** Sal. Arch. 34/2, f. 77.

MICHAEL BURKE took the oath in Santiago on 17 March 1755 and on 8 September 1757 in Salamanca. He sat examinations on 22 August 1758 and 30 August 1759 and was pronounced 'very satisfactory'. For his third year examination on 23 June 1760 he showed 'want of study'. He received minor orders in Santiago on 17 June 1757 from Archbishop Bartolomé Rajoy. He left for Ireland from Bilbao in June 1760.[42]

RICHARD BURKE entered the Irish College in Santiago on 26 December 1638.[43]

THEOBALD BURKE, an Irish priest and a licentiate, in his application for financial aid to pursue his studies in 1626 stated that he had been a student of the Irish seminary in Santiago and later in Salamanca, where he completed his studies. He had been attending the University of Alcalá for the past year (1625) and wished to graduate before returning to Ireland. The Irish College in Alcalá de Henares was not founded until 1649, although there had been an earlier college founded in 1630 by John O'Neill third earl of Tyrone and son of the great Hugh O'Neill. Burke claimed to be the superior of a group of Irish students in the University of Alcalá.[44]

THOMAS BURKE entered the college in 1657 and paid 70 *reales*. He was presented for minor orders by rector William Salinger in Santiago on 16 September 1660.[45]

WALTER BURKE took the oath on 17 March 1755 in Santiago and in Salamanca on 8 September 1757. He received minor orders (*prima y grados*) on 17 June 1757 from Bishop Bartolomé Rajoy. In Salamanca he passed first and second examinations on 22 August 1758 and 30 August 1759 and gave very good proof of application. On 23 June 1760 in the third year examination, together with the other candidates he showed lack of study. John O'Brien, rector of Salamanca, certified that on 25 June 1760 Walter Burke with six other collegians left for Ireland from the port of Bilbao, all of them priests for the Irish mission. Each of them was given 100 ducats from 'His Catholic Majesty.'[46]

---

42 Sal. Arch. I/3, XXIII/I/ii; *Arch. Hib.* 4, pp 9, 40; Couselo, op. cit., p. 25. 43 Sal. Arch. 34/2, f. 34 v.   44 Micheline Kerney Walsh, 'The Irish College of Alcalá de Henares', *Sea. AM* 11:2 (1985), pp 249–50, 253–4.   45 Sal. Arch. XXIII/2, 34/2, f. 57 v.   46 Couselo, op. cit., p. 25. Sal. Arch. I/3, XXIII/I/ii; *Arch. Hib.* 4, pp 9, 40. All the students did badly at the third year examination on 23

JAMES (SANTIAGO) BUTLER took the oath on 17 March 1740 in Santiago and was presented for minor orders, no date given. In Salamanca on 17 May 1742 he swore the oath and passed his first year examination on 29 August 1743 and the second year on 28 July 1744. He did well in the third examination on 23 June 1745. He was ordained in September 1743, having received minor orders in Santiago de Compostela on 9 April 1741. He left for Ireland in June 1745.[47]

JOHN BUTLER received minor orders on 21 March 1724 in Santiago. He took the oath in Salamanca on 6 July 1724 and sat the second year examination there in 1725 and was approved.[48]

WILLIAM BUTLER took the oath on 17 March 1737 in Santiago and in Salamanca on 12 September 1739. He sat for second year theology on 22 August 1740 and was singled out for special praise. He was back in Ireland by 1742.[49]

CABAXNAH *see* KAVANAGH

RICHARD CAFFREY took the oath in Santiago on 17 March 1711.[50]

FRANCIS CAHILL was in Santiago on 23 October 1761, had a ledger account there and took the oath there on 17 March 1764, 1765 and 1766 and in Salamanca on 21 June 1766 and was ordained on 13 June 1767. He left for Ireland 27 May 1770.[51]

PETER CAHILL, *licenciado*, from Cashel archdiocese, signed the oath in Salamanca in December 1652. He was taken into the Salamanca college for one year by the rector, according to a document dated 1652. His patent had been presented in Santiago by rector Ignatius Lombard on 16 December 1650.[52]

CANTY *see under* MOLINA.

CARNEY *see also* KEARNEY

June 1760 and alleged 'want of time on account of the new chair of Controversies in which they were not examined on account of the illness of the master from 24 May'. **47** Sal. Arch. I/3, XXIII/I/ii, XXIII/42; *Arch. Hib.* 4, pp 7, 29, 30, 31; Couselo, op. cit, p. 24. **48** Couselo, op. cit., p. 23; *Arch. Hib.* 4 pp 5, 26. **49** Sal. Arch. I/3, XXIII/I/ii; *Arch. Hib.* 4, p. 7, 29. **50** Sal. Arch. XIII/I/ii. **51** Sal. Arch. XXIII/I/ii, 34/7 *Arch. Hib.* 4, pp 11, 45, 47. **52** Sal. Arch. XXIII/2; *Arch. Hib.* 3, pp 107–8.

JAMES PHILIP CARNEY SJ (or O'Kearney) was from the the diocese of Cashel, son of Philip Carney and Helen Saul, born 1601 and was in the Irish College, Santiago in 1617. He was a nephew of Fr Barnaby O'Kearney SJ. He paid 76 and 400 *reales* for his brother, John, and himself and signed the oath in Salamanca on 22 July 1620.[53]

JOHN CARNEY, brother of the above, was also in the college in 1617.[54]

CARTHY, CARTY *see* MAC CARTHY

PATRICK CARY arrived in Salamanca from Santiago in October 1697 and was examined the following year on 1 October in first year theology and passed on to second theology.[55]

THOMAS CASEY from Limerick city was one of the students in the college at the time (1631) of the enquiry re Felix O'Neill, student. On 28 July 1631 he was under 26 years of age and was an ordained priest. He signed a statement about Felix O'Neill on 28 July 1631 during the investigation.[56]

JOSEPH CAVALLERS was ordained as sub-deacon on 23 December 1690, deacon on 10 March 1690 and *de misa* (to the priesthood) on 31 March 1691 by Archbishop Monroy in Santiago.[57]

CAVOOD *see* CAWOOD

MICHAEL CAWOOD SJ, born 23 June 1707 in Dublin, is entered in the Santiago college ledger of personal accounts (*Libro de Quentas Particulares*) for the cost of items of clothing, possibly 1724. He took the oath in Santiago on 17 March 1725. He received minor orders (*de prima y menores*) on 24 February 1725, having been presented by rector Joannes Henriques SJ two days before. He was received into the Society in Seville in 1726 and ordained in 1737 and was in the Irish College, Seville until 1738. He returned to Dublin in 1738 and was assigned to St Mary's Lane Chapel and died in 1772.[58]

CIENFUEGOS *see* KEATING

---

53 Sal. Arch. 34/2, f. 10, v.11; *Arch. Hib.* 3, pp 93–4. Finnegan, op. cit., p. 143. **54** Sal. Arch. 34/2, f. 10 v. **55** *Arch. Hib.* 4, p. 22. **56** Sal. Arch. 33/1/15. Information about the Felix O'Neill enquiry will be found in Chapter 6; *Knights*, iii, 4. **57** Couselo, op. cit., p. 23. **58** Sal. Arch. XXIII/I/ii, XXIII/2, 34/7; Rev. J.J. Silke, *Arch. Hib.* 24, (1961) 'The Irish College, Seville', p. 128. Couselo, op. cit., p. 24. Finnegan, op. cit., p. 25, says he was a convert to Catholicism.

CLEAR *see* CLERY

JOHN (O) CLERY SJ, born in Waterford 20 September 1624, entered the Irish College, Santiago on 5 February 1640. He paid 970 *reales*. He entered the Society 2 July 1641 and was ordained 1650. In 1659 the procurator of the college was John Clery. John Clear from Waterford was prefect of studies in Santiago in 1658 and returned to Ireland in 1660. He was attached to the Waterford residence 1671–6. He died on 23 May 1684.[59]

JEROME CLINTON took the oath in Santiago on 17 March 1710. He went on to Salamanca where he was ordained before 1 April 1715, the date on which he signed *in verbo sacerdotis* that he had fulfilled his obligations to say two masses each week for the *limosna* (offering) received from the rector. In 1713 Jerome Clinton was one of the only four students in the college at that time. He was given very high praise for his performance in his examination in 1713 and high encomium of his talents and intelligence in 1714. He left for the Mission in 1715.[60]

JOHN CODD (COAD) took the oath in Santiago 17 March 1734. He had arrived with a companion, Patrick Redmond, by mule from Tuy. He was a paying boarder and deposited sums of money, including 11 *doblones*, for himself and Redmond. When he arrived he was suffering from a troublesome itch, or *sarna* and had to get special treatment for it. He was presented for minor orders in Santiago on 29 April 1735 by rector Araujo. He went on to Salamanca and took the oath there on 16 May 1736. He had left for Ireland in 1742.[61]

JOHN COLEMAN took the oath in Santiago on 17 March 1747 and in Salamanca on 17 March 1749. He did very well at his first year examination on 26 August 1749 and on 31 August for his second year his result was middling. He was sent out of the college without a letter of recommendation in March or May in 1751. He was one of those involved in the Sheehy episode in the Irish College, Salamanca. There was a Fr John Coleman, parish priest of Dunderry, Co. Meath, who died on 15 March 1767. Could this be the same John Coleman?[62]

---

59 Sal. Arch. S 34/2 ff. 35, 58. Finnegan, op. cit., p. 27.   **60** Sal. Arch. XXIII/I/ii; *Arch. Hib.* 4, p. 4, 24.   **61** Sal. Arch. I/3, XXXIII/I/ii, XXIII/2, 34/7; *Arch. Hib.* 4, p. 7; Tuy is south of Santiago, near the Portuguese border.   **62** Sal. Arch. XXXIII/I/ii; *Arch. Hib.* 4, p. 8, 34; *Meath Index*, p. 1228. Some details on the Sheehy episode will be found in Chapter 6.

WILLIAM COLLYN from Bannow, Co. Wexford, son of John Collin and Mariane Sinnott, entered the Irish College in Santiago on 7 December 1617 and paid 300 *reales*. He studied philosophy there until he went to Salamanca in 1620. He went back to Ireland as an ordained priest in 1624.[63]

JAMES COMERFORD went to Alcalá de Henares from Santiago in 1649 when that college was set up. He may have been born Kilkenny 1630 and entered the Society in 1650, returned to Ireland 1676 and was stationed n Kilkenny; he was arrested and transported to Poitiers.[64]

MATHEW COMERFORD may have been a student in Lisbon in 1613. He paid the sum of 400 *reales* in Santiago in 1614.[65]

THOMAS COMERFORD received minor orders (*prima y menores*) on 2 March 1703, sub-deacon on 2 June 1703, a deacon on 24 August 1703 and ordained to the priesthood (*de presbítero*) in September 1703.[66]

JOHN CONIGAN came from Santiago to Salamanca in October 1670. He had not been examined before leaving Santiago but was approved by the examiners in Salamanca. On 13 October 1671 he was examined and approved for second year theology.[67]

JEREMIAH CONNELL took the oath in Santiago on 17 March 1725 and in Salamanca on 14 May 1727. For first year theology he was examined and approved on 26 September 1728 and for second year on 27 July 1729. He was billed in the college ledger in Santiago *c*.1725 for clothing and tobacco. In July 1730, having finished his studies, he left for Ireland.[68]

THOMAS (O) CONNERY took the oath in Santiago on 17 March 1758 and in Salamanca on 20 July 1760.He was presented for minor orders on 12 June 1760 in Santiago. He sat the first year examination on 8 October 1761, the verdict being that he answered 'less than middlingly'; in the second year he was examined on 4 September 1762 and found unsatisfactory. He was pronounced 'wretched all round' on 10 May 1763 when he sat the third year examination. He left for Ireland about this time.[69]

---

63 Sal. Arch. S 34/2, f. 11, 40/2; *Arch. Hib.* 3, p. 91. **64** Arnáiz-Sancho, p. 61, 87–8; Finnegan, op. cit., p. 30. **64** Sal. Arch. S 34/2, f. 10. He is not listed by me in *The Irish College at Lisbon, 1590–1834*. **66** Couselo, op. cit., p. 23. **67** *Arch. Hib.* 4, p. 18. **68** Sal. Arch. XXIII/I/ii and 34/7; *Arch. Hib.* 4, pp 6, 26. **69** Sal. Arch. XXIII/I/ii, XXIII/2; *Arch. Hib.* 4, pp 10, 41, 42. He is found also as O'Connery, Sal. Arch. XXIII/2, when presented for minor orders on 12 June 1760.

JOHN PATRICK CONROY paid 400 *reales* when he entered Santiago on 7 December 1617. Could be Patrick Conway, born Cashel 1605, entered the Society 1625, ordained 1635 and was stationed at Cashel for nineteen years?[70]

JOHN CONWAY SJ, son of Peter Conway and Elizabeth Saule, from the archdiocese of Cashel, studied philosophy in the Irish College, Santiago before going to Salamanca where he swore his oath on 4 June 1620. He was then aged about 22 years. He was received into the Society in Seville in 1622, and was stationed at Cashel from 1630. He died there in 1642.[71]

CORNELIO *see* O'CONNOR

JOHN RICHARD CROSBY contributed *una limosna* of 400 *reales* in Santiago in 1667. He came to Salamanca in October 1670 and he swore his oath on 1 November 1671 and passed his second year examination on 13 October 1671 and on 2 October 1672 sat his third year examination.[72]

JOHN CRUISE swore the oath in Santiago on 16 April 1713.[73]

JOHN CULLEN took oaths in Santiago and Salamanca on 17 March 1762 and 17 July 1763.[74]

PATRICK CURTIS (1) arrived in Salamanca in October 1679. He had been examined and approved in Santiago before leaving there. In Santiago he had paid 4004 *reales* for outfitting and maintenance in 1676 and additional amounts, including £50 English money, for his *alimentos* during his time there.[75]

PATRICK CURTIS (2) was from Meath diocese. He took the oath in Santiago on 17 March 1728. He was examined in Salamanca, approved for second year on 27 July 1729 and pronounced a choice student. In his third year examination on 31 August 1730 he received a high encomium. He was not the future rector of Salamanca (1780–1817) but was a kinsman of his. He was born *c.*1705 in Flemingstown, Co. Meath, and became tutor to the sons of the Duque de Osuna and also his chaplain in 1744.[76]

70 Sal. Arch. S 34/2, f. 11; Finnegan, op. cit., p. 33. 71 *Arch. Hib.* 3, p. 93; Finnegan, op. cit., p. 32. 72 *Arch. Hib.* 3, p. 108; 4, p. 18; Sal. Arch. 34/2, f. 72. 73 Sal. Arch. XXIII/I/ii. 74 Sal. Arch. XXIII/I/ii; *Arch. Hib.* 4, p. 10. 75 *Arch. Hib.* 4, p. 20; Sal. Arch. 34/2 ff 82, 84 and 87. 76 Sal. Arch. XXIII/I/ii; *Arch. Hib.* 4, pp 26–7; Micheline Kerney Walsh, 'The Irish College of Madrid', *Sea. AM* 15:2 (1993), p. 48. The Duque de Osuna, a descendant of '*el gran duque de Osuna*', belonged to one of the premier noble houses of Spain.

GEORGE CUSACK took his oath in Santiago on 9 October 1704. On 21 March 1707 in Salamanca he swore to observe the *Condiciones.*[77]

DALAIT *see* DALY

DALY *see also* O'DALY

PETER DALY from the diocese of Clonfert was a student in Santiago before Febuary 1646 when he swore his oath in Salamanca. He was involved in Santiago in the *pleito* regarding Fr Sherlock's library. He took an examination in Salamanca in November 1647 and gave 'a good account' of himself. He received his viaticum of 300 *reales* in 1648.[78]

GODFREY DANIEL was from Co. Galway. He was sent from Santiago to Alcalá de Henares when that college was founded in 1649 and was the first rector of the Irish College in Alcalá de Henares. He later became rector of the Irish College in Madrid and was there in 1652.[79]

WILLIAM DARDIS from the diocese of Meath took the oath in Santiago on 6 January 1644 and in Salamanca on 11 February 1646. In November 1647 he was examined in Salamanca and given a good report. He took part with Peter Daly in the *pleito* regarding Fr Sherlock's library.[80]

JAMES DAVIN SJ took the oath in Santiago on 17 March 1725. He received minor orders on 24 February. He appears in the college ledger for expenses incurred including some pictures for his bedroom and the hire presumably of a mule in *c.*1725. He was apparently well-off and even paid the overtime fee of 6 *reales* extra to have a tailor work on his outfit at night. His letters to rector John O'Brien (Salamanca) and others written from Madrid from 1740 to 1756 are interesting. He was born in Waterford 11 November 1704

77 Sal. Arch. XXIII/I/ii; *Arch. Hib.* 4, p. 23, see also *Arch. Hib.* 3, pp 108–10 for a note on the *Condiciones.* **78** *Sal. Letters* 13/AA/1/7 p. (Sal. Arch. XIII/7); *Arch. Hib.* 3, pp 99–102; 4, p. 14. Some detail on Fr Sherlock's library is to be found in Chapter 3. Dardis and Davy initiated the *pleito* or lawsuit about the library after Fr Sherlock's death, lost it and were both considered troublesome by the rectors in Santiago and Salamanca. See also *Arch. Hib.* 3, pp 99–107 which is in part about real or perceived conflict between Connacht students and the authorities in Salamanca, that is the Irish Jesuits, mainly from Munster in 1648. **79** Arnáiz-Sancho, pp 61, 87–9. M. Kerney Walsh, 'The Irish College of Madrid', *Sea. AM* (1993), p. 42. **80** Sal. Arch. XXIII/I/i, 34/2, f. 62 v; *Arch. Hib.* 4, p. 14. & ibid., 3, p. 103.

and was a nephew of Fr Thomas Gorman SJ. He died in Madrid on 28 July 1760.[81]

WILLIAM DEASY (Desio) was in Santiago in 1660 and paid 100 *reales* on entry towards his outfitting. He went from Santiago to Salamanca in May 1664, having been examined in Santiago before leaving. In 1667 he stayed on for a fourth year of theology in Salamanca and was not examined as he was known to have sufficient knowledge.[82]

FRANCIS DELAMOR SJ went from Santiago to Alcalá when that college was founded in 1649. He is possibly the Jesuit born in Dublin on 4 October 1626 who entered the Society 12 May 1650 and was ordained 1656.[83]

ANTHONY DEVEREUX from Waterford was received in Santiago on 11 January 1652 aged 20 years. He was son of William Devereux and Maria Sharpe and was educated by the Jesuits. He deposited the sum of 80 ducats when he arrived. He may be Anthony Devereux who was born on 4 February 1632, entered the Society in Portugal on 22 January 1658 and was sent to Angola.[84]

PETER DEVEREUX took the oath on 17 March 1743 in Santiago and on 1 August 1745 in Salamanca. He arrived in Salamanca from Santiago in July 1745. He passed his first year examination on 16 July 1746 but 'answered badly because of his poor intelligence', according to rector John O'Brien. He did better in 1747 and 'midddlingly' in 1748. He left for Ireland on 25 June 1748.[85]

RICHARD DEVEREUX, who also appears as John Richard Devereux, took the oath on 17 March 1728 in Santiago. He received minor orders (*tonsura y menores*) in Santiago on 17 March 1729. He swore his oath in Salamanca on 27 November 1730. He was examined and approved on 25 July 1732 in second year theology in Salamanca.[86]

JAMES DEVINE took the oath in Santiago on 18 March 1767 and arrived in Salamanca in November.

---

81 Sal. Arch. XXIII/I/ii, XXIII/2, 34/7; *Sal. Letters*, pp 231–3, XV/D/5/1 – XV/D/5/17 (Sal. Arch. XV/1–17); Couselo, op. cit., p. 24; Finnegan, op. cit., p. 41. **82** *Arch. Hib.* 4, pp 17, 18; Sal. Arch. 34/2, f. 62 v. **83** Arnáiz-Sancho, pp 61, 87–8; Finnegan, op. cit., p. 41. **84** Sal. Arch. XXIII/I/i; Finnegan, op. cit., p. 43. **85** Sal. Arch. XXIII/I/ii; *Arch. Hib.* 4, pp 7, 31, 32, 33. **86** Sal. Arch. XXIII/I/ii; *Arch. Hib.* 4, pp 6, 27, 28; Couselo, p. 24.

DIXEREUX *see* DEVEREUX

BARTHOLOMEW DONALDSON, paid 143 *reales* for his *vestuario* on 17 October 1656.[88]

THADEUS DONOVAN paid a *limosna* of 270 *reales* in 1667.[89]

CHRISTOPHER DONNELLY took oath in Santiago on 17 March 1755 and in Salamanca on 8 September 1757 and he was examined there in August 1758 and 1759. He received minor orders on 17 June 1757 from Bishop Bartolomé Rajoy in Santiago. He left in June 1760 from Bilbao for Ireland.[90]

PATRICK DORAN took the oaths in Santiago and Salamanca on 17 March 1755 and 8 September 1757 and was examined on 22 August 1758 and was pronounced very satisfactory. On 30 August 1759 he was examined for second year theology; on 23 June 1760 for third year. The second year results were very good in 1759 but for the third year showed 'want of study' in June 1760. He had received minor order (*prima y grados*) on 17 June 1757 in Santiago. He left for Bilbao to return home on 25 June 1760.[91]

JAMES DOWDALL took the oath in Salamanca on 14 May 1727 and was examined in first year theology on 26 September 1728 and approved. He was debited for clothes in Santiago, possibly in 1725. On 27 July 1729 he sat his second year examination and his result was excellent. He signed a petition to the king on 16 February 1729 in Salamanca. In July 1730, having finished his studies, he left for the Mission.[92]

BERNARD DOWNES took oaths on St Patrick's Day in 1746 and in 1749 in the Santiago and Salamanca Irish Colleges respectively. H also signed the *Condiciones* on 24 April 1750. He was ordained in Santiago in minor orders (*prima y grados*) by Bishop Gil Taboada on 14 November 1747. He left Salamanca without a letter of recommendation as he had been also involved in the Sheehy episode.[93]

DENIS DOYLE took the oath 1711 in Santiago on St Patrick's Day and in Salamanca 1 April 1715 and left the same year for the mission. He was apparently a priest when he came from Ireland to Spain. He was said to be

---

87 Sal. Arch. XXIII/I/ii, 52/5/14; *Arch. Hib.* 4, p. 46.   88 Sal. Arch. 34/2, f. 54. 89 Sal. Arch. S34/2, f. 72.   90 Sal. Arch. I/3, XXIII/I/ii; *Arch. Hib.* 4, pp 9, 40; Couselo op. cit., p. 25.   91 Sal. Arch. I/3, XXIII/I/ii; *Arch. Hib.* 4, pp 9, 40; Couselo, op. cit., p. 25.   92 Sal. Arch. 34/7; *Arch. Hib.* 4, pp 6, 26, 27.   93 Sal. Arch. XXIII/I/ii; *Arch. Hib.* 4, pp 8, 34; see fn. 62 above; Couselo, op. cit., p 25.

'of extraordinary talent' and he received a high encomium at his examination in Salamanca on 28 September 1714.[94]

JOHN IGNATIUS DOYLE took the oath on 17 March 1730 in the Irish College, Santiago.[95]

LAURENCE DOYLE took the oath in Santiago on 17 March 1728 and in Salamanca on 27 November 1730. The rector objected to his being passed in examination because he had arrived from Santiago without the customary certificate. This was overruled. A letter, in Spanish, from the archbishop of Dublin not permitting him to Holy Orders and revoking his *dimissorias* is dated 9 August 1731. He was examined in second year on 25 July 1732 and approved.[96]

WILLIAM DOYLE took the oath on 17 March 1737 in Santiago and on 12 September 1739 in Salamanca. He was examined in second year theology on 22 August 1740 and was approved. He was back in Ireland by 1742.[97]

DIRSCOLL *see* O'DRISCOLL

EDWARD DRUMGOOL from Killartry, Clogherhead, Co. Louth, was in Santiago in 1664 and paid 40 *reales* for his outfit. He came back to Salamanca from Santiago as a licenciate on 22 September 1667 and took the oath there on 30 October 1667. He was vicar-general of the diocese of Clogher until Dr Duffy was appointed in 1671. He was described by St Oliver Plunkett in 1673 as 'one of the best priests I have'. After the martydom of Archbishop Plunkett he was appointed vicar apostolic of Armagh.[98]

JOHN DRUMGOOL SJ paid the sum of 1,794 *reales* in Santiago in 1676 for maintenance for two years and for his outfitting.[99]

BERNARD EGAN (signed Bernardus de Egano) took the oath in Santiago on 21 September 1631. He was a friend of Felix O'Neill.[100]

See Chapter 6 re Sheehy episode.   **94** Sal. Arch. XXIII/I/ii; *Arch. Hib.* 4, pp 4, 24.   **95** Sal. Arch. XXIII/I/ii.   **96** Sal. Arch. XXIII/I/ii; *Arch. Hib.* 4, pp 6, 27, 28; *Salamanca Letters,* p. 6 (XIII/5; 13 AA 1 35) omitted from listing on page 6. **97** Sal. Arch. I/3, XXIII/I/ii; *Arch. Hib.* 4, pp 7, 29.   **98** *Arch. Hib.* 3, p. 108; 4, p. 18; Sal. Arch. 34/2, f. 67; Donnchadh MacPhoil, 'The clergy of Oliver Plunkett', *Sea. AM,* 11:1 (1983/4), pp 49–52,   **99** Sal. Arch. S 34/2, f. 84v. Finnegan, op. cit., p. 49.   **100** Sal. Arch. XXIII/I/i, 33/I/15.

MILETIUS (MILESIUS WILLIAM) ELLICOTT took the oath in Santiago on 17 March 1728, and in Salamanca on 27 November 1730. He was approved on 25 July 1732 in second year and pronounced as of good quality and application. He was ordained in minor orders on 17 March 1729 in Santiago by Bishop José de Yermo y Santibáñez.[101]

CHRISTOVAL DE EMPO was a student in Santiago and paid 200 *reales* in 1623.[102]

RICHARD ENGLAND entered Santiago on 8 Febrary 1640 and signed the oath on 11 October 1640. He was 22 years old. He brought 720 *reales* in cash and *en letra* (letter of credit?).[103]

BARNABY ESMONDE (EDMUNDUS MAC EAMOINN) was from the diocese of Ferns. He was presented for minor orders by the rector, Ignatius Lombard, on 16 December 1650 in Santiago. He took the oath in Salamanca on 8 December 1652.[104]

NICHOLAS EVERARD came from Santiago to Salamanca in October 1670 and was approved there at that time and for his second year on 13 October 1671.[105]

PATRICK EVERARD SJ from Armagh diocese was received in the college in Santiago 2 May 1670, aged 20. He was son of Edward Everard and Eulamia Brady. He paid a *limosna* of 100 *reales* between himself and Patrick Molano (Mullan, in 1670). He went from Santiago to Salamanca in 1673 and was examined and approved for first and second year theology on 14 October 1673 and 1 October 1674 in Salamanca.[106]

PETER EVERARD SJ, paid 96 *reales* for his habit and other necesssities in 1664 in Santiago. He arrived as a licentiate in Salamanca on 22 September 1667 and had been examined and approved before leaving Santiago.[107]

PETER FAGAN paid two amounts, 3,200 and 1,600 *reales* for *alimentos y vestuario* in Santiago. These were to cover two years, 1675 and 1676, and his outfitting.[108]

---

101 Sal. Arch. XXIII/I/ii; *Arch. Hib.* 4, pp 6, 27, 28; Couselo, op. cit., p. 24. **102** Sal. Arch. S. 34/2, f. 17.   **103** Sal. Arch. XXIII/I/1, 34/2, 35.   **104** Sal. Arch. XXIII/2; *Arch. Hib.* 3, p. 108.   **105** *Arch. Hib.* 4, p. 18.   **106** Sal. Arch. XXIII/i/i, 34/2, f. 77; *Arch. Hib.* 4, p. 19.   **107** *Arch. Hib.* 4, p. 18; Sal. Arch. 34/2, f. 67. Finnegan, op. cit., p. 53.   **108** Sal. Arch. 34/2, ff.79v, 82.

FAI *see* FAY

DANIEL FALLON was sent to the Irish College, Alcalá de Henares in 1649.[109]

GREGORY FALLON was from the diocese of Cloyne. He took the oath in Santiago on 15 December 1637 and in Salamanca on 16 October 1639. He was a sponsor for a knighthood of Calatrava for Hugo Eugenio O Neill in 1644 in Madrid.[110]

NICHOLAS FALLON paid for food in Santiago in 1688 and was ordained on 10 March 1691 in Santiago by Archbishop Monroy. He was examined and approved in Salamanca on 1 October 1692. He is referred to as Nicholas Falon, theologian in the Salamanca record. Some records of sponsorship for knighthoods in 1694, 1709 and 1722 include a Fr Nicholas Fallon. Birthplace is given variously as Connacht, Galway and Clare.[111]

RICHARD FALLON took the oath in Santiago on 9 October 1631. He was in the college during the Felix O'Neill investigation. A Dr Richard Fallon, canon of Murcia, sent sums of money to the college in 1692. He died in Malaga *c*.1701. A legacy is recorded after his death and the college received 500 and 280 *reales* in 1706.[112]

JAMES FANIN paid 520 *reales* for food and outfitting in *c*.1679.[113]

PATRICK FAY took oath in Santiago 17 March 1752, and arrived in Salamanca on 27 June 1754. He was examined for first year, and did very well on 26 August 1755. Rector John O'Brien wrote that he would have been the best in the second year examination but he was ill at the time and recovering in the summer residence (Aldearubia) on 22 August 1756. Having done his final examination on 22 June 1757, he left for Ireland four days later. He had received minor orders in Santiago from Bishop Carlos Antonio Rional, bishop of Mondoñedo, no date given.[114]

---

109 Arnáiz-Sancho, pp 61, 87–8.   **110** Sal. Arch. XXIII/I/i; *Arch. Hib.* 3, p. 98; he was in the Irish College, Santiago in 1636 when he witnessed Patrick Fleming's signature – Sal. Arch. XXIV/I. Micheline Kerney Walsh, *Spanish knights of Irish origin*, vols 1–4 (Dublin, 1960–78), ii, p. 106.   **111** Couselo, op. cit., p. 23; Sal. Arch. 34/2, f. 104v; *Knights*, ii, p. 7, iii, p. 32; iv, p. 6.   **112** Sal. Arch. XXIII/I/i, 33/1/1, 34/2, ff. 109, 129 v.140, 150. The Felix O'Neill investigation is detailed in Chapter 6.   **113** Sal. Arch. 34/2, f. 88.   **114** Sal. Arch. XXII/I/ii; *Arch. Hib.* 4, pp 38, 39; Couselo, op. cit., p. 25.

DOMINIC FAYON (FINE?) went to Alcalá de Henares from Santiago in 1649.[115]

HUGH FAYON was born in Oranmore, Co. Galway, and was a sponsor for knighthood of Arturo O Broin in Madrid in 1696. He came from Santiago to Salamanca before October 1689. He was examined and approved for third year theology on 2 October 1690 in Salamanca. He was ordained in minor orders on 15 September 1687 by Archbishop Monroy in the chapel of the archbishop's palace in Santiago.[116]

GERALD FENNEL, student in Santiago, paid 424 *reales* in 1623.[117]

EUGENE FIELD OFM is listed by O'Sullivan Beare as a student in Santiago prior to 1613 who became a Franciscan, and had qualified in Theology and Preaching.[118]

NICHOLAS FIELDING in 1664 he paid for habits and other necessities. The name is also given as Fillingo.[119]

THADY FINN took the oath in Santiago three times, in 1764, 1765 and 1766, and in Salamanca on 22 June 1766. He was ordained on 24 September 1768 by the bishop of Salamanca and left for Ireland on 27 May 1770.[120]

RICHARD FITZGERALD (GERALDINO) was a student who paid to the college 314 *reales* in October 1617 and also in 1619 when additional funds came to him from Ireland.[121]

THOMAS FITZGERALD (GERALDINO) was in Santiago prior to 1613 and according to Patrick Sinnott served in Flanders. He is also listed by O'Sullivan Beare and was the heir to the Lord of the Vale. The Lord of the Vale (Valle) was one of the cadet branches of the earldom of Desmond: a fourteenth-century earl instituted a series of knighthoods (Knight of Glyn, of Kerry, of Lixnaw, etc.).[122]

RICHARD FITZPATRICK received minor orders and took the oath in Santiago on 17 March 1740. He swore the oath in Salamanca on 16 May 1742. He was examined there on 29 August 1743 and approved in first year,

115 Arnáiz-Sancho, pp 61, 87–8. 116 *Arch. Hib.* 4, pp 20, 21; Couselo, op. cit., p. 23; *Knights*, iii, p. 32. 117 Sal. Arch. 34/2, f. 17. 118 Sal. Arch. 33/1/15. 119 Sal. Arch. 34/2, f. 67. 120 Sal. Arch. XXIII/I/ii; *Arch. Hib.* 4, pp 11, 45, 46, 47. 121 Sal. Arch. 34/2, ff. 10, 11v. 122 Sal. Arch. 35/4, 33/1/15.

for second year on 28 July 1744 and third on 23 June 1745 and did badly at both of these latter examinations. He was ordained in December 1743 and by 25 June 1745 he had left for the mission. [123]

JAMES FLANNOLIS (FLAGOLLIS, FLANNELLY) from diocese of Killala took oath in Santiago on 15 October 1637 and in Salamanca on 16 October 1639. He was a sponsor in 1644 for Hugo Eugenio O Neill for award of knighthood of Calatrava.[124]

PATRICK FLEMING was in the college in Santiago on 3 August 1635 and until 19 September 1636 when he left for health reasons. He was an ordained priest and had come to the college to study Arts. He received a viaticum of 150 *reales de vellón* when he was leaving. Gregory Fallon witnessed his signature on 19 September 1636.[125]

MARCOS FLETCHER paid 300 and 404 *reales* in Santiago for maintenance in 1672 and 1673.[126]

EDWARD FLOOD is probably Edward Folo who paid 100 *reales* when he entered the seminary *c.*1670.[127]

THOMAS FLOOD took the oath on 17 March 1761 in Santiago and in Salamanca on 17 July 1763. Flood was examined for first year on 25 August 1764 and pronounced very good, and for second year on 29 August 1765 with the verdict that he was very satisfactory. He left to sail from Bilbao on 11 April 1766 with Thomas Molloy.[128]

RICHARD FORTEL paid 200 *reales* in 1668 in the Irish College at Santiago.[129]

EDWARD FORD took the oath in Santiago on 18 March 1730 or 1731 and in Salamanca on 18 May 1733. He was examined and approved on 29 July 1734 in first year theology, and on the same date in 1735 in second year theology he was judged to have excellent ability. He had been ordained in minor orders (*de corona y grados*) by Bishop José Yermo y Santibáñez in Santiago on 25 March 1733. In Santiago, according to the ledger, he paid his personal account with three *doblones*.[130]

123 Sal. Arch. I/3, XXIII/I/ii, XXIII/2; *Arch. Hib.* 4, pp 7, 29, 30, 31.   **124** Sal. Arch. XXIII/I/i; *Knights,* ii, p. 106; *Arch. Hib.* 3, p. 98.   **125** Sal. Arch. XXIV/I. **126** Sal. Arch. 34/2, f. 79. v.80.   **127** Sal. Arch. 34/2, f. 77.   **128** Sal. Arch. XXIII/I/ii; *Arch. Hib.* 4, pp 10, 43, 45.   **129** Sal. Arch. 34/2, f. 74 v.   **130** Sal. Arch. XXIII/I/ii, 34/7; *Arch. Hib.* 4, pp 6, 28, 29; Couselo, op. cit., p. 24.

JOHN FOYES was ordained by Bishop Yermo y Santibáñez *de corona y grados* on 25 March 1733 in Santiago.[131]

MARK FOYO from Connacht was a collegian in Santiago who died on 23 September 1736 and was buried in the college church of the Society of Jesus where Fr Domingo Bolaño, with twelve priests, carried out the funeral service.[132]

GREGORY FRENCH took the oath on 17 March 1710 in Santiago; he was examined in Salamanca on 27 September 1713 and on 28 September 1714 and a very good account of him given. He left Spain for Ireland in April 1715. A gold ring which he had deposited with the rector was returned to him at that time. He wrote *in verbo sacerdotis* that he had said all masses for which he had received offerings [133]

MARTIN FRENCH came to Salamanca from Santiago and was examined and approved for lectures in theology in June 1649.[134]

DANIEL GAFFNEY paid 100 *reales* in the Irish College, Santiago in the period *c.*1678/9.[135]

JOHN GARLON paid 175 *reales* for food in the college in the years 1676/7 or 1678/9.[136]

GERALDINO *see* FITZGERALD

JAMES GOGGIN took the oath in Santiago on 17 March 1719.[137]

ANGELO GOLDEN was sent from Santiago to Alcalá de Henares in 1649.[138]

THOMAS GORMAN SJ took the oath in Santiago on 17 March 1710 and sat examination in Salamanca on 27 September 1713. He was stated to have 'extraordinary talent'. He was son of Edmund Gorman and Margaret Meagher, born in Clonmel 29 December 1691. He entered the Jesuits in March 1714 and was ordained 1621. He was recalled to Ireland in 1724, spent four years at Clonmel. In 1721 he was sent to Limerick and then to Cork. Eventually he went to Poitiers in 1761. He was expelled from France when the Society was suppressed and lived in Spain until 1767 when the Society was expelled from that kingdom. He died near the Gulf of Corsica on 19 June 1767 and was buried at sea. His handwriting is beautiful.[139]

---

131 Couselo, op. cit., p. 24. 132 Ibid., 34–5. 133 Sal. Arch. XXIII/I/ii; *Arch. Hib.* 4, pp 4, 24. 134 *Arch. Hib.* 4, p. 15. 135 Sal. Arch. 34/2, f. 84 v. 136 Ibid. 137 Sal. Arch. XXIII/I/ii. 138 Arnáiz-Sancho, pp 61, 87–8. 139 Sal. Arch.

RICHARD GRACE took the oath on 9 October 1704 in Santiago.[140]

JOHN GRANE entered the college in April 1639 and paid 165 *reales*.[141]

THOMAS GREGORY paid the sum of 300 *reales* in 1623.[142]

JAMES HACKETT took the oath on 17 March 1740 in Santiago and in Salamanca on 16 May 1742. He was ordained *de órdenes menores* (minor orders) on 9 April 1741 in Santiago. He went on to Salamanca and was examined and approved in first year there on 29 August 1743. He did third year examination on 23 June 1745. He did badly in his examinations. He was ordained a priest in February 1744 and left for the mission before 25 June 1745. He was drowned at sea. There is a letter from him to rector O'Brien dated 16 March 1743.[143]

THOMAS HAGIL (or Haie) was in the college *c*.1631 at the time of the Felix O'Neill investigation.[144]

MICHAEL HALE (or Hail) took the oath on 17 March 1752 in Santiago.[145]

HALIBET *see* ALERVET

DANIEL HANGLIO or HAUGLIO OFM (Anglim) was in the college in Santiago prior to 1613; according to O'Sullivan Beare he became a Franciscan.[146]

PATRICK HANLY took the oath in Santiago on 10 October 1704 and in Salamanca on 21 March 1707 where he swore to observe the *Condiciones*. He was examined in second year on 28 September 1708 and approved to pass into third year. He left for Ireland on 20 May 1709.[147]

THOMAS HANRAHAN from Clonmel, Co. Tipperary took the oath in Santiago on 19 January 1612; he was then aged 19 years. His parents were Gibons Kiramdum Hanrechan and Elizabeth White.[148]

JOHN HARRISON SJ born in Gorey on 28 September 1682, signed the oath in Santiago on 2 April 1705. There was a letter from his uncle, Thomas Harrison, Gorey, dated 10 October 1726 and addressed to him as rector of

XXIII/I/ii; *Arch. Hib.* 4, p. 24; Finnegan, op. cit., pp 65–6. **140** Sal. Arch. XXIII/I/ii. **141** Sal. Arch. 34/2, f. 35. **142** Sal. Arch. 34/2, f. 17. **143** Sal. Arch. I/3, XXIII/I/ii, XXIII/2, 34/7; Couselo, op. cit., p. 24; *Arch. Hib.* 4. pp 7, 29, 30, 31; *Sal. Letters*, 13 AA 1 53, p. 7. **144** Sal. Arch. 33/1/15. **145** Sal. Arch. XXIII/I/ii. **146** Sal. Arch. 33/1/15. **147** Sal. Arch. XXIII/I/ii; *Arch. Hib.* 4, p. 23. For details of *Condiciones* see *Arch. Hib.* 3, pp 108–11. **148** Sal. Arch. XXIII/I/i.

Salamanca. At the time of the letter his mother, a sister and a brother named Richard were alive. He was rector of Santiago (1724–8) and later of Salamanca (1728–30). He was a brother of another Jesuit, Fr James Harrison (1695–1768). He died in 1738.[149]

PHILIP HASSET came to Salamanca from Santiago in November 1769, the year the rector did not permit the collegians to attend the University. In October 1770 he began his second year course. On 13 April 1773 he left for Ireland.[150]

HAUGLIO *see* HANGLIO

MICHAEL HEALY arrived from Santiago in Salamanca on 27 June 1754. He was ordained by the bishop of Salamanca, José Zorilla, in St Martin's on either 17 or 24 November 1755. His examination results were not satisfactory or only middling on 26 August 1755, 22 August 1756 and 22 June 1757. He left for Ireland on 26 June 1757.[151]

JOHN HELAN entered Santiago in 1657 and paid 58 *reales*.[152]

EDMUND HENNESSY arrived in Santiago before March 1740 where he signed the oath. He was also presented for minor orders and had a ledger account. He swore the oath in Salamanca on 16 May 1742. He was approved in the first year examination on 29 August 1743; the second year on 28 July 1744 was not great; but the third year on 23 June 1745 was satisfactory. He left for Ireland two days after his last exam on 25 June 1745.[153]

JAMES HENNESSY was presented by rector Araujo for minor orders (no date). He had a ledger account in 1734 in Santiago. He went on to Salamanca and took the oath there on 16 May 1736. In his first year examination on 4 August 1737 he was approved to the great satisfaction of the examiners.[154]

MICHAEL HENNESSY swore the oath in Santiago on 17 March 1749 and in Salamanca on 12 September 1751. He received minor orders in Santiago probably on 14 April 1751. In his first year examination on 26 August 1752

149 Sal. Arch. XXIII/I/ii; *Sal. Letters,* 13 AA 1 25, p. 5 (XIII/25); Finnegan, op. cit., pp 71–3; *IER,* William McDonald (May 1874), p. 114. 150 Sal. Arch. 52/5/14; *Arch. Hib.* 4, pp 46, 48, 49. 151 *Arch. Hib.* 4, pp 38, 39; Couselo, op. cit., p. 25. 152 Sal. Arch. 34/2, f. 57 v. 153 Sal. Arch. I/3, XXIII/I/ii, XXIII/2, 34/7; *Arch. Hib.* 4, pp 7, 29, 30, 31. 154 Sal. Arch. XXIII/2, 34/7; *Arch. Hib.* 4, pp 7, 29. 155 Sal. Arch. XXIII/2, XXIII/I/ii; *Arch. Hib.* 4, pp 8, 36, 37.

he was pronounced 'excellent', in second year on 21 August 1753 he showed 'ability and application', and in third year on 17 June 1754 he did very well. He left for Ireland ten days later.[155]

PHILIP HIRE took the oath in Santiago on 16 December 1650.[156]

PHILIP HOLLAND (the name is also written Olano, Guolano, Huolano, O'Houlaghan) was in the college before September 1613 when he went to Salamanca. He was a student of jurisprudence in the University of Santiago, the son of Denis Holland and Cecilia Carty, and was 22 years old in 1613. He was from Birhaven in the diocese of Ross.[157]

EDWARD HORE (Duarte Hox) from Aughafad, Co. Wexford, son of Denis Hore and Katherine Hay. He was three years in Santiago before going to Salamanca and took the oath there in 1617. In April 1613 in Santiago he paid, with John Brodir, 510 *reales* for their outfits.[158]

JAMES HORE (1) paid a *limosna* of 144 *reales* in 1667 in Santiago.[159]

JAMES HORE (2) was examined and approved in Santiago before leaving for Salamanca where he arrived in October 1676. He took the oath there on 10 September 1677. He was a witness to the oath of Richard Lynch in 1673 in Santiago. Are these two distinct James Hores or one and the same seminarian?[160]

NICHOLAS HORE SJ from Aghfadd, Co. Wexford, diocese of Ferns, entered the seminary in Santiago on 10 February 1640 and paid 117 *reales*. Born *c.*1620, he was son of David Hore and Elizabeth Roche. He went on to Salamanca for his theology and entered the Jesuits sometime before 17 March 1646. He died on 1 November 1649.[161]

HOULANUS *see* HOLLAND

JAMES HOWARD took the oath on 17 March 1764, 1765 and 1766 in Santiago and in Salamanca on 22 June 1766. He left for Ireland on 27 May 1770, having completed his studies.[162]

FELIX HUGHES took the oath in Santiago on 17 March 1734 and in Salamanca on 16 May 1736. He gave a good account at his first year

156 Sal. Arch. XXIII/2. **157** Sal. Arch. 35/4, 33/1/15; *Arch. Hib.* 2, p. 30. **158** *Arch. Hib.* 2, pp 34/35; Sal. Arch. 34/2, f. 5. **159** Sal. Arch. 34/2, f. 72. **160** *Arch. Hib.* 3, p. 111; 4, p. 19; Sal. Arch. XXIII/I/i. **161** Sal. Arch. I/2, 34/2, f. 35; Cat. MSS. Hib. SJ, 1556–1669, p. 334. **162** Sal. Arch. XXIII/I/ii; *Arch. Hib.* 4, pp 11, 45, 47.

examination on 4 August 1737. He received minor orders on 20 October 1734 in Santiago.[163]

JAMES HUGHES signed the oath on 17 March 1758 in Santiago and in Salamanca on 20 July 1760. His examination results were good for first year on 8 October 1761, for second year on 4 September 1762 and for third year on 23 June 1763. He said his first mass on 25 March 1762 (?), having been ordained by the bishop of Salamanca.[164]

RAYMOND HUSSEY was in the college in Santiago before 1613. According to Sinnott's list there were two Husseys in the college. The Christian name of the other collegian is not given by him. One died and the other became a secular priest and returned to Ireland. O'Sullivan Beare lists a Raymond Hussey whom he says was a jurist.[165]

THOEBALD JONES was from Cregmore, Co. Mayo, diocese of Tuam, a son of Richard Jones and Anaplam Theobaldi. He studied humanities in Santiago under Fr James Oualle SJ. His name is found as Jonyn. He took the oath in Salamanca in 1620 when he was 23 years old.[166]

JAMES JOYCE (his name is found as Jacobo Josillo and Joseo) paid 600 *reales* in 1673 in Santiago for food for eight months and 600 as *limosna*.[167]

JOHN JOYCE paid 4 doubloons for his outfitting which included gloves. He took the oath on St Patrick's Day 1731 in Santiago and on 18 May 1733 in Salamanca. He had been examined and approved in Santiago. He was pronounced excellent in Salamanca on his first and second year examination on 29 July in 1734 and 1735.[168]

MARK JOYCE entered Santiago on 31 March 1735 and paid for his board in the college until October 1736. He took the oath there on 17 March 1736.[169]

BERNARD KAVANAGH took the oath in Santiago on 17 March 1752 and in Salamanca on 8 September 1755. He had received ordination in minor orders (*de prima y grados*) in Santiago from Carlos Antonio Riomol, bishop of Mondoñedo, with testimonials of rector Araujo. He was ordained to the priesthood with others on 17 and 24 November 1755 by the bishop of Salamanca, José Zorilla, in St Martins.[170]

---

163 Sal. Arch. XXIII/I/ii, XXIII/2; *Arch. Hib.* 4, pp 7, 29.   164 Sal. Arch. XXIII/I/ii, XXIII2; *Arch. Hib.* 4, pp 10, 41, 42.   165 Sal. Arch. 33/I/15, 35/4.   166 *Arch. Hib.* 3, p. 93.   167 Sal. Arch. 34/2, pp 79, 80; Finnegan, op. cit., p. 76.   168 Sal. Arch. XXIII/I/ii, 34/7; *Arch. Hib.* 4, pp 6, 28, 29.   169 Sal. Arch. XXIII/I/ii, 34/7.   170 Sal.

JOHN KEAGHRY swore the oath on 17 March 1761 in Santiago and in Salamanca on 16 July 1763. His report was good for the first year examination on 25 August 1764; he answered well, in the second year on 29 August 1765. He defended *Dominicales* on 19 May 1765 in the Royal College and got an extra special supper there. He was ordained on 21 December 1765 with a dispensation in age and left from Bilbao for Ireland on 1 June 1766.[171]

PHILIP KEARNEY swore his oath on 17 March 1743 in Santiago.[172] See also CARNEY or O'CARNEY

EDWARD KEATING (CIENFUEGOS) SJ, born on 1708 in Wexford, took the oath on 17 March 1731 in Santiago and in Salamanca on 25 May 1734. It would appear that he was already an ordained priest in Santiago. There is a good account of his examinations for first year theology on 29 July 1735 and for second year on 29 July 1736. He was parish priest of Wexford from 1756 until his death in 1777.[173]

WALTER KEATING was presented for minor orders possibly on 14 April 1751 in Santiago and swore the oath on 17 March 1749 in Santiago and in Salamanca on 12 September 1751. There is a good account of his examinations on 26 August 1752, 21 August 1753 and 17 June 1754. He left for Ireland 27 June 1754.[174]

KIEREVAN *see* KIRWAN

RICHARD KELLY was ordained in minor orders (*prima y menores*) on 21 March 1724 in Santiago. He took the oath in Salamanca on 6 July 1724. He was examined for his second year theology and approved on 26 September 1725. He was also approved in his third year examination on 27 September 1726. He probably left in July 1727 for Ireland.[175]

DENIS KENNEDY from the diocese of Cashel, son of Donald Kennedy and Finula Hogan was in the college in Santiago before 1617 when he came to Salamanca and swore the oath on 14 April. He was examined in Salamanca on 7 April and approved. According to a note by rector Briones in the Irish

Arch. XXIII/I/ii; *Arch. Hib.* 4, pp 9, 38; Couselo, op. cit., p. 25.   **171** Sal. Arch. XXIII/I/ii; *Arch. Hib.* 4, pp 10, 43, 44, 45.   **172** Sal. Arch. XXIII/I/ii.   **173** Sal. Arch. XXIII/I/ii, 34/7; *Arch. Hib.* 4, pp 7, 29; M. Foley, *The Past*, 8 (1970), p. 11. **174** Sal. Arch. XXIII/I/ii, XXIII/2; *Arch. Hib.* 4, pp 8, 36, 37; *The Past*, 8 (1970), p. 11. **175** Couselo, p. 23; *Arch. Hib.* 4, pp 25, 26.

College, Salamanca Kennedy graduated as a BA in the University of Salamanca on 13 May 1617.[176]

DANIEL KEOGH was in Santiago in 1660 and 1661 and arrived in Salamanca from there in May 1664. He had been examined in Santiago before leaving.[177]

ANDREW KIERAN entered the seminary in Santiago on 26 December 1638.[178]

BRENARD KIERNAN paid 500 *reales* when he was received as a *colegial* in 1666.[179]

JAMES KIERNAN (QUERNANO) arrived in Salamanca in October 1676 having been examined and approved in Santiago. He paid various sums for his keep in Santiago from about 1673. He donated a house to the college which has already been mentioned. A Fr James Kiernan from Cavan was sponsor in 1682 for a knighthood of Calatrava for Joseph King.[180]

JOHN KINIGAN paid a donation of 198 *reales* in 1667 in Santiago.[181]

AUGUSTUS KIRWAN (KIEREWAN) took the oath in Santiago on 17 March 1743 and in Salamanca on 1 August 1745, having arrived there in July. There is a good account of his examinations in July 1746 for first year and on 12 August 1747 for second year. He also defended *Dominicales* in the Royal College in April 1747. He was ordained in Avila in December and returned to Ireland in June 1748. He was described as 'talented and of angelical habits'. There is a very good report on him by the rector.[182]

FRANCIS KIRWAN was ordained *de prima y menores* 24 February 1725. He swore the oath in Salamanca on 14 May 1727. He is debited for clothes and supplies, including tobacco, in the college ledgers. In Salamanca there is a good report on his examinations on 26 September 1728, but on 27 July 1729 his result is reported as 'middling'. Having finished his studies he left for Ireland in July 1730.[183]

JOHN KIRWAN (QUIROVANO) paid 300 *reales* for board in Santiago c.1676. He arrived in Salamanca in October 1679, having been examined and approved in Santiago.[184]

176 *Arch. Hib.* 2, p. 35; 4, p. 12.   **177** *Arch. Hib.* 4, p. 17; Sal. Arch. 34/2, f. 63. **178** Sal. Arch. 34/2. f. 34 v.   **179** Sal. Arch. 34/2, f. 70.   **180** *Arch. Hib.* 4, p. 19; Sal. Arch. 34/2. f. 79; *Knights*, iii, p. 24.   **181** Sal. Arch. 34/2, f. 72.   **182** Sal. Arch. XXIII/I/ii; *Arch. Hib.* 4, pp 7, 31, 32, 33.   **183** Couselo, op. cit., p. 24; Sal. Arch. 34/7; *Arch. Hib.* 4, pp 5, 26.   **184** *Arch. Hib*, 4, p. 20; Sal. Arch. 34/2, f. 84 v.

THOMAS KIRWAN (1) took the oath in Santiago on 17 March 1746 and in Salamanca on 17 March 1749. His examination records are 'very good' in first year on 26 August 1749 and in second year he did 'middlingly' on 31 August 1750; his writing is very decorative. He was involved in the Sheehy episode and was expelled on 18 March (?) 1751. He was ordained in minor orders (*prima y grados*) in Santiago on 14 November 1747.[185]

THOMAS KIRWAN (2) swore the oath on 17 March 1752 in Santiago and in Salamanca on 7 October 1756. He had arrived in Salamanca on 27 June 1754 and did 'middlingly' in the first year examination on 26 August 1755. He did well in the second year examination on 22 August 1756; in third year he was examined on 22 June 1757; although he was reported to have ability he showed lack of application. On 26 June he left for Ireland.[186]

WILLIAM KUGANCIO entered the college in Santiago on 10 November 1639 and he and Bartholomew Read paid 150 *reales*.[187]

STEPHEN LAMPORT was ordained on 2 March 1703 *de prima y menores* by Bishop Monroy and on 24 August 1703 as sub-deacon, deacon on 4 September 1703 and finally *de misa* (priesthood) on 17 March 1704.[188]

WILLIAM LAMPORT, from the diocese of Ferns, was presented by rector Barnaby Bath SJ, Irish College, Santiago, for minor orders with his patent on 25 May 1706.[189]

PETER NICHOLAS LANGTON SJ, from the city of Kilkenny, diocese of Ossory, paid 470 *reales* when he came to Santiago on 7 December 1617. He was son of Nicholas Langton and Laetia Daniel. He studied philosophy for three years in Santiago before going to Salamanca on 3 June 1620 when he was aged 25 years. He was ordained 20 July 1620, and entered the Society in 1622.[190]

FRANCISCO LEA was a student in the Irish College, Santiago in 1623 and paid 400 *reales* to the college.[191]

NICHOLAS GEORGE LEA paid 300 *reales* in Santiago on 7 December 1617.[192]

---

185 Sal. Arch. XXIII/I/ii; *Arch. Hib.* 4, pp 8, 34; Couselo, op. cit., p. 25. See Chapter 6 for details on the Sheehy episode. **186** Sal. Arch. XXIII/I/ii; *Arch. Hib.* 4, pp 9, 38. **187** Sal. Arch. 34/2, f. 35. **188** Couselo, op. cit., p. 23. **189** Sal. Arch. XXIII/2. **190** Sal. Arch. 34/2, f. 11; *Arch. Hib.* 3, p. 91; Finnegan, op. cit., p. 84. **191** Sal. Arch. 34/2. f. 17. **192** Sal. Arch. 34/2, f. 11.

WILLIAM LEA paid 440 *reales* in Santiago in 1623.[193]

THOMAS LEARY SJ (Lereo). Thomas Leneus paid a *limosna* of 100 *reales* when he entered Santiago in 1670. A Thomas Lereo entered first year in the Irish College, Salamanca on 14 October 1673 having come from Santiago. Fr Finnegan lists Thomas Leary, born Cashel 1655, who entered the Society 1674. He died in 1691.[194]

PETER LENETE (LEVET); his signature appears to be Petrus Lenete, but could be Peter Levet. He took oath in Santiago on 24 March 1658. Nine freshmen arrived in Salamanca from Santiago in 1658: all the others went back to Ireland 1661 except Peter Levet, who was not old enough for ordination, so he had to spend another year in the seminary. He was examined in September 1659 and was approved. However, he is referred to as Fr Lenete in 1659.[195]

JOHN LEONARD. 120 *reales* cash was received in 1614 on his behalf in the Irish College, Santiago. He was born Waterford 1599 and entered the Society in 1616.[196]

MATHEW LEONARD came to the college from Ireland in 1624 and paid 550 *reales*.[197]

LINCAEUS *see* LYNCH

LINCE *see* LYNCH

JAMES LINCOLN came to the Santiago college in 1624 and paid 400 *reales*.[198]

RICHARD LINCOLN was afterwards archdeacon of Glendalough and archbishop of Dublin. He took the oath in Santiago on 17 March 1725, having entered on 8 June 1724, and in Salamanca on 14 May 1727. On 26 September 1728 he was examined for first year theology and gave very good account of himself. On 27 July 1729 he was examined and approved – 'excellent' – for third year. He had been ordained de *prima y menores* (*minor orders*) on 24 February 1725. In July 1730, having finished his studies, he left for Ireland.[199]

---

193 Sal. Arch. 34/2, f. 17. **194** *Arch. Hib.* 4, p. 19; Sal. Arch. 34/2, f. 7; Finnegan, op. cit., p. 89. **195** Sal. Arch. XXIII/I/i; *Arch. Hib.* 4, pp 16, 17, in the Salamanca records in *Arch. Hib.* he is referred to as Peter Levet. **196** Sal. Arch. 34/2, f. 10; Finnegan, op. cit., p. 88. **197** Ibid., f. 18. **198** Sal. Arch. 34/2, f. 18. **199** Sal. Arch. XXIII/I/ii, XXIII/2, 34/7; *Arch. Hib.* 4, pp 6, 26; Couselo, op. cit., p. 24;

EDWARD LISWARD SJ was born in Cashel on 1 February 1715, son of Hugo Lisward and Kathleen Morris. He took the oath on 17 March 1736 in Santiago. He was ordained a sub-deacon on 21 February 1739 by Bishop Lorenzo Taranco Muvaurieta in the Irish College, Santiago. He had entered the college on 22 September 1734 and paid his keep up to December of that year. His oath in Salamanca was dated 6 May 1739. In 1764 he returned to Ireland and served in the Augustinian house, John's Lane, Dublin, and was renowned for his sermons. He worked in Dungarvan from 1750 to 1761. He was already a priest when he was received into the Society of Jesus. He returned to Spain as rector of Salamanca, 1761–4. He died in Dublin 1791.[200]

JAMES NICHOLAS LOMBARD paid 200 *reales* on 7 December 1617 in Santiago.[201]

WILLIAM LOMBARD was, according to C. Pérez Bustamente, a collegian in the Irish College, Santiago de Compostela and a Latin poet with poems printed and dedicated to the Conde-Duque de Lerma in 1633. He was in the college during the Felix O'Neill investigation, was 18 years old in 1631 and was from the city of Wexford.[202]

WILLIAM LONERGAN took the oath on 17 March 1761 in Santiago and in Salamanca on 17 July 1763. His first year examination was weak. He was expelled, taken back and on 12 June 1765 expelled again. He was ordained to the priesthood in March 1765 by auxiliary Bishop Zelanese. In the same year a Fr William Lonegan from Carrick, Co. Tipperary, is cited as a sponsor for a knighthood.[203]

NICHOLAS LOVELOCK took the oath on 17 March 1734 in Santiago and in Salamanca on 16 May 1736. He gave a good account of himself in the first year theology examination and was approved on 4 August 1737 and also in his second year on 18 August 1738. He was presented in Santiago by rector Araujo for minor orders (no date given). He also had an account in the ledger in the Irish College, Santiago. He had left for the mission sometime before 1742.[204]

Knights, ii, p. 61; *Rep. Novum*, 2: 1 (1958), pp 211–12.   **200** Sal. Arch. XXIII/I/ii, XXIII/2, 34/7; *Arch. Hib.* 4, p. 7; Couselo, p. 24. Bishop Taranco was auxiliary of Orozco and bishop of Abaren. See also Finnegan, op. cit., p. 91.   **201** Sal. Arch. 34/2, f. 11.   **202** Sal. Arch. 33/1/15. C. Pérez Bustmente et al., *La universidad de Santiago, el pasado y el presente* (Santiago, 1934), p. 31.   **203** Sal. Arch. XXIII/I/ii; *Arch. Hib.* 4, pp 10, 43, 44; *Knights*, ii, p. 27.   **204** Sal. Arch. 1/3, XXIII/I/ii,

ANDREW LYNCH swore the oath on 17 March 1728 in Santiago, and in Salamanca on 1 December 1730. He was approved on his second year examination on 25 July 1732. He had received minor orders in Santiago on 17 March 1729.[205]

COLUMBANUS (Columba) LYNCH was in Santiago in 1670 and paid 100 *reales* as *limosna*. He signed the oath in Salamanca on 17 March 1671. He was approved for second year theology on 1 October 1674. He signed the certificate to say mass for the rector's intentions in 1676 in Salamanca.[206]

MARK LYNCH SJ entered Santiago in 1670 and paid a *limosna* of 100 *reales*. He was approved to enter first year theology on 18 October 1673 when he arrived in Salamanca. He entered the Society in 1673. He was born in Galway in 1651. He was a priest by 1681. He returned to Galway in 1687/88 after the fall of the city to the Williamites. He was deported from there to France and died in that country in 1726.[207]

MATHEW LYNCH. In 1657 the sum of 78 *reales* was received for the habit of this student in Santiago. He took the oath there on 25 March 1658. He was examined and approved in Salamanca on 30 September 1659 and on 5 October 1660. He left for Ireland in 1661.[208]

MICHAEL LYNCH came to Salamanca from Santiago in 1692 where he had been examined and began theology. He signed an oath in Salamanca on 17 March 1697. On 3 October 1697 he was examined and approved for first year and on 1 October 1698 he was examined in second year theology and approved to pass on to third year.[209]

PATRICK LYNCH SJ (1) was a nephew of Fr Richard Lynch SJ, who around the year 1657 paid 400 *reales* for his nephew's outfit. He is referred to as *hermano* (brother) Patricio Linze. Is he Patrick Lynch SJ born in Galway on 27 October 1640 who entered the Society in March 1657, was ordained 1666–7, was recalled to Ireland on 30 April 1689 and was appointed

---

XXIII/2, 34/7; *Arch. Hib.* 4, pp 7, 29. **205** Sal. Arch. XXIII/I/ii; *Arch. Hib.* 4, pp 6, 27, 28; Couselo, op. cit., p. 24. **206** *Arch. Hib.* 3, pp 108, 110; 4, p. 19; Sal. Arch. 34/2, f. 77. **207** *Arch. Hib.* 4, p. 19; Sal. Arch. 34/2, f. 77; Finnegan, op. cit., 95–6. **208** Sal. Arch. XXIII/I/i, 34/2, f. 55; *Arch. Hib.* 4, pp 16–17. **209** *Arch. Hib.* 3, p. 112; 4, pp 21, 22. There appears to be a divergence between 1692 and 1697 in the records of this student: he is supposed to have come to Salamanca in 1692 but does not take first year examination there until 1697.

superior of the Jesuit mission in Ireland 1689? He died in Dublin 6 February 1694.[210]

PATRICK LYNCH (2) paid 384 *reales* in 1673 or 74 in Santiago and took the oath there on 17 March 1674. In Salamanca he swore his oath on 10 October 1677, having arrived there from Santiago in October 1676. The seal on his oath is very clear: Compostellani Collegii Ibernorum.[211]

RICHARD LYNCH paid 600 *reales* for eight months' maintenance c.1672. He was from Co. Roscommon, son of Patrick Lynch and Juliana French. He was 23 years old in 1673 when he took the oath in the Irish College, Santiago de Compostela. The signature on his oath was witnessed by Thady Ryan and James Hore. He arrived in Salamanca in October 1676 and had been examined and approved in Santiago.[212]

LYNZE *see* LYNCH

CHARLES (MAC) CARTHY. His name is given as Carty. He was 22 years old in 1613. He was a lay student in the Irish College, Santiago in 1613 when the Jesuits took over its government.[213]

FLORENCE (MAC) CARTHY (1) His name is given as Carty and he was also a lay student in the college in 1613, studying jurisprudence in the University. According to Sinnott he went to the Court 'a pretender' (to solicit funds) and thence to Flanders where he died.[214]

FLORENCE MAC CARTHY (2) signed the oath in Santiago on 17 March 1758. He took minor orders on 12 June 1760. A Florence Mac Carthy is listed in Salamanca at the second year theology examination on 4 September 1762 and answered well. He did not present himself for examination on 8 October 1761 'on pretext of illness'. In June 1763 he answered very well at the third year examination.[215]

PATRICK MAC DONELL from diocese of Meath took the oath on 17 March 1713 in Santiago and in Salamanca on 4 October 1715. He signed as Patricius McDonel. He was probably already a priest before coming to Spain. He was one of the only two students in the college in 1716 and was

210 Sal. Arch. 34/2, ff. 54, 55. Finnegan, op. cit., pp 196–7. Details of Fr Richard Lynch, Finnegan, op. cit., p. 98. **211** Sal. Arch. XXIII/I/i, 34/2, f. 80; *Arch. Hib.* 3, p. 111; 4, p. 19. **212** Sal. Arch. XXIII/I/i, 34/2, ff. 79; *Arch. Hib.* 4, p. 19. **213** Sal. Arch. 33/1/15. 35/4. **214** Ibid., 35/4. **215** Sal. Arch. XXIII/I/ii, XX/III/2. *Arch. Hib.* 4, pp 41, 42.

examined in the three theology courses: the verdict was *supra mediocritis*. He was also examined on 28 September 1718 and the verdict was very good. He went on the mission the same year.[216]

MAC EAMONN *see* Esmonde.

MAC GHEE *see* MAGEE

JAMES MC GIRR from Co. Tyrone took the oath on 29 September 1676 in Santiago. His parents were Patrick McGirr and Catherine Ni Dohoty; his teachers in Ulster were all Jesuits. He was 19 years old in 1676. His oath was witnessed by Paul Wadding and Barnaby Bathe.[217]

MORIARTACH MAC GUEGAN paid 300 *reales* on 7 December 1617 in Santiago.[218]

JAMES MC MAHON, signed the oath on 17 March 1725 and received minor orders in Santiago on 24 February 1725. He was debited for clothes in the college ledger about this time. He was son of Constantine and Honoria McMahon, born Armagh 25 July 1704, who entered the Soceity 22 October 1725. He lived in Limerick 1738 and died there 1753.[219]

JAMES MC MULLEN swore the oath on 17 March 1728 in Santiago. In Salamanca he was approved for second year theology on 27 July 1729 He was considered a choice student. For the third year examination he got high encomium on 31 August 1730. He signed a petition with others to the king on 16 February 1729.[220]

THOMAS MC PARLAN took the oath on 17 March 1749 in Santiago and was presented for minor orders by rector Araujo, possibly on 14 April 1751. He swore the oath in Salamanca on 12 September 1751. His examination results were poor. He left for Ireland on 27 June 1754.[221]

FELIX MAGEE took the oath on 17 March 1734 in Santiago and in Salamanca on 16 May 1736. He was approved for first year theology examination on 4 August 1737. He was presented for minor orders in Santiago on 20 October 1734 and appears in the ledger charged 3 *pesos* to buy a breviary.[222]

---

216 Sal. Arch. XXIII/I/ii; *Arch. Hib.* 4, pp 5, 24.   **217** Sal. Arch. XXIII/I/i. **218** Sal. Arch. 34/2, f. ll.   **219** Sal. Arch. XXIII/I/ii, XXIII/2, 34/7; Couselo, op. cit., p. 24; Finnegan, op. cit., p. 106.   **220** Sal. Arch. XXIII/I/ii; *Arch. Hib.* 4, pp 26, 27. No details of the petition given.   **221** Sal. Arch. XXIII/I/ii, XXIII/2; *Arch. Hib.* 4, pp 8, 36, 37.   **222** Sal. Arch. XXIII/I/ii, XXIII/2, 34/7; *Arch. Hib.* 4, pp 7,

JAMES MAGUIRE paid 300 *reales* for his outfitting sometime between 1675 and 1678.[223]

THOMAS MAGUIRE signed oath on 17 March 1761 in Santiago and in Salamanca on 16 July 1763. He was examined for first year theology on 25 August 1764 and was dubbed 'weak'; on 29 August 1765 for the second year examination he was pronounced as answering 'middlingly'. He was ordained to the priesthood in March 1765 by the auxiliary bishop, Zelanese. He left for home via Bilbao on 11 March 1766.[224]

MALONE *see* MOLONO

MANNIN *see* O'MANNING

MARTIN MARLEY took the oath on 17 March 1707 in Santiago. He arrived in Salamanca on 19 September 1709. His third year examination result was very good on 28 September 1711 and he left for home in May or June 1712.[225]

JEREMIAH MARTIN from Galway took the oath in Santiago on 22 November 1670. He was 19 years of age and his signature was witnessed by John Bodkin. He was approved for first year theology on 14 October 1673 in Salamanca and for second year on 1 October 1674. He was son of Thomas Martin and Juliana Bodkin. He swore an oath in Salamanca on 17 March 1674.[226]

PATRICK MATERSON, from the diocese of Kilmore, took the oath on 17 March 1737 in Santiago and in Salamanca on 12 September 1739. He was pronounced very good after his second year examination on 22 August 1740. He was debited for clothes for going to La Coruña in early October 1738. He was back in Ireland in February 1742 in charge of the parish of Cavan. He sent a letter from Paris in 1755 to rector John O'Brien in Salamanca which contains interesting information about the college and other clerics there in his time. He was parish priest of Cavan and died in 1782.[227]

NICHOLAS MAYLES was ordained *de prima y menores* on 2 March 1703 in Santiago, as sub-deacon on 2 June, deacon on 24 August and *de misa* on 24 September 1703 by Archbishop Monroy.[228]

---

29.   **223** Sal. Arch. 34/2, f. 84 v.   **224** Sal. Arch. 34/2, f. 84 v.   **225** Sal. Arch. XXIII/I/ii; *Arch. Hib.* 4, pp 23, 24.   **226** Sal. Arch. XXIII/I/i, 34/2, f. 77; *Arch. Hib.* 3, p. 111; 4, p. 19.   **227** Sal. Arch. 1/3, XXIII/I/ii, 34/7, 52/5/9; *Arch. Hib.* 4, pp 7, 29; *Breifne*, 6 (1986), p. 314.   **228** Couselo, op. cit., p. 23.

MEACHAR *see* O'MEAGHER

MERYNINE(A) *see* MURNANE

MOLANO *see* MULLIN

PATRICK MOLANO (Mullan) paid 100 *reales* in Santiago in 1670 with Patrick Everard. He arrived in Salamanca in October 1673 and was approved to enter first year theology. A Fr Patrick Molano, from Dublin, was sponsor for candidates for knighthoods in 1678, 1682 and 1687.[229]

CANTY MOLINA (could be Mullen, Miller or the surname could be Canty or Carty); this collegian was a Bachelor of Arts, prior to 1613. He complained in a petition to Philip III about the house in Santiago in the La Huerta quarter (*barrio de las Huertas*). The mayor confirmed that the house '*no es cómodo ni suficiente*' (neither comfortable nor adequate). The king acceded to the petition but there was no action taken on it. Richard Conway in 1616 rented a house in the Rua Nova for the college and in 1620 bought it from the university for 1,020 ducats. This house, no. 44 Rua Nova, is still standing in Santiago.[230]

ARTHUR MOLLOY took the oath on 17 March 1725 in Santiago. He had entered the college on 22 August 1724 and his outfit was charged against him in the college ledger, his keep for 56 days and 60 *reales* for the man who delivered his trunk. His oath in Salamanca was taken on 14 May 1727.[231]

THOMAS MOLLOY took the oath on 17 March 1762 in Santiago and on 16 July 1763 in Salamanca. His examination record was good in first year on 25 August 1764 and second year on 29 August 1765 he answered well and the verdicts were 'very satisfactory'. He was ordained to the priesthood on 1 April 1766 by the bishop of Salamanca. He left for home with Thomas Flood via Bilbao on 11 April 1766.[232]

MALACHY MOLONO, a priest, was presumably a student in the college in Santiago where he paid the sum of 400 *reales*, with Jeremiah de Burgo in 1617/18.[233]

---

229 Sal. Arch. 34/2, f. 77; *Arch. Hib.* 4, p. 19; *Knights*, iii, pp 22, 24, 27.　**230** Sal. Arch. 35/4; he is listed by Sinnott who says he returned to Ireland and married there. Riviera, op. cit., pp 432, 433.　**231** Sal. Arch. XXIII/I/ii, 34/7; *Arch. Hib.* 4, p. 6.　**232** Sal. Arch. XXIII/I/ii; *Arch. Hib.* 4, pp 10, 43, 45.　**233** Sal. Arch. 34/2, f. 10v.

WALTER MOLONEY (also found as Moloriney, Mulrooney, Mullowny) took the oath on 18 March 1767 in Santiago. He went on to Salamanca and arrived there in November 1769, which was the year the rector there did not permit the students to attend the university. He left for Ireland on 13 April 1773.[234]

MOLONEY *see also* MOLONO

ANDREW MORGAN arrived in Santiago on 27 September 1733 without a patent from the provincial of the Jesuits in Ireland. He took the oath on 17 March 1734 in Santiago and in Salamanca on 16 May 1736. In Santiago he was debited for clothes and food and was very ill, and his brother, Patrick, who lived in Bilbao, paid his expenses. In Salamanca he took his first year examination on 4 August 1737 and his second year on 18 August 1738 and was reported to be 'good'. He left for Ireland in 1742.[235]

NICHOLAS MORRIS swore the oath on 17 March 1749 in Santiago and on 13 September 1751 in Salamanca. He was examined for first year theology on 26 August 1752 and was pronounced as 'excellent' and for second year on 21 August 1753 as 'very good'. He was ordained to the priesthood on 31 March 1754 and on 13 April defended *Conclusiones* in theology in the Royal College. On 17 June 1754 he was examined for third year and did very well. He left for Ireland on 27 June 1754.[236]

JOHN MULLALY was debited with 170 *reales vellón* in Santiago and presented for minor orders by rector Araujo, undated. He took the oath in Salamanca on 16 May 1736; he was examined on 4 August 1737 for first year theology and for second year on 18 August 1738 and merited a good verdict in both examinations.[237]

NICHOLAS MULLIN took the oath on 18 March 1767 in Santiago and arrived in Salamanca in November 1769, the year the rector in Salamanca did not allow the students to attend the university. He left for Ireland with viaticum and testimonials on 30 June 1774.[238]

MURNANE *see* MURNINE

234 Sal. Arch. XIII/I/ii, 52/5/14; *Arch. Hib.* 4, pp 46, 49.   235 Sal. Arch. 1/3, XXIII/I/ii, XXIII/2, 34/7; *Arch. Hib.* 4, pp 7, 29.   236 Sal. Arch. XXIII/I/ii, XXIII/2; *Arch. Hib.* 4, pp 8, 36, 37.   237 Sal. Arch. XXIII/2, 34/7; *Arch. Hib.* 4, pp 7, 29.   238 Sal. Arch. XXIII/I/ii, 52/5/14; *Arch. Hib.* 4, pp 46, 49.

EDWARD MURNINE(A) (MERYNINE) came to Salamanca from Santiago in June 1710 and gave evidence of his proficiencey. At his third year theology examination on 28 September 1711 he was reported to have given a very good account. He returned to Ireland in June 1712.[239]

EDMUND MURPHY (1) from Birhaven was 20 years old in 1631. He was in the college during the Felix O'Neill episode.[240]

EDMUND MURPHY (2) was in Santiago in 1664 and paid 400 *reales* for outfitting and board.[241]

EDWARD MURPHY was in Santiago in 1673 when he paid 435 *reales* for his *vestuario y alimentos* for some months before the course began. He arrived in Salamanca from Santiago in October 1676 having been examined and approved before leaving Santiago. He signed an oath on 10 October 1677 in Salamanca.[242]

JOHN MURPHY was the famous Fr Murphy, parish priest in Dublin. He took the oath in Santiago on 17 March 1728, and in Salamanca on 27 November 1730. He was examined for second year on 25 July 1732 and approved and praised for good ability and application. There is a letter from him in Dublin, 1752, to the rector written by order of the archbishop of Dublin, Dr Linegar, regarding the Sheehy affair, dated 30 January 1752.[243]

PETER MURPHY paid 22 and a half *pesos*, equal to 565 *reales*, for outfitting and board in *c.*1679.[244]

THOMAS MURPHY took the oath on 17 March 1737 in Santiago, in Salamanca on 6 May 1739 and was examined and approved in second year theology on 22 August 1740.[245]

JOHN NUGENT was a *licenciado* (BA or licentiate) from the Meath diocese. He took the oath on 24 February 1649 in Santiago. He came to Salamanca at the beginning of June 1649 and took the oath there on 6 October 1650. He was approved to attend lectures in theology. On 23 September 1650 and on 26 October 1651 he was examined and gave a good account of the material studied. He left for Ireland after 28 May 1652.[246]

---

239 *Arch. Hib.* 4, pp 23, 24; *Sal. Arch.* 1/3.   240 Sal. Arch. 33/i/15.   241 Sal. Arch. 34/2, f. 67.   242 *Arch. Hib.* 3, p. 111; 4, p. 19; Sal. Arch. 34/2, f. 79 v. 243 Sal. Arch. XXIII/I/ii; *Arch. Hib.* 4 pp 6, 27, 28; *Sal. Letters,* 13 AA 1 105, p. 12. 244 Sal. Arch. 34/2, f. 88.   245 Sal. Arch. XXIII/I/ii; *Arch. Hib.* 4, pp 7, 29. 246 Sal. Arch. XXIII/1/i; *Arch. Hib.* 3, pp 106, 107; 4, p. 15.

DANIEL O'BRIEN paid 200 *reales* to the college in Santiago when he arrived there in 1614.[247]

HUGO O'BRIEN was in Santiago in 1662 and paid 120 *reales* for his habit. He arrived in Salamanca from Santiago May 1664 and had been examined and approved in the latter college.[248]

JAMES O'BRIEN was in Santiago in 1658. He refused to go on the mission and was suspended from saying mass. The rector, William Salinger, in a letter to the Provisor or vicar general asks that he should be ordered to leave Santiago immediately.[249]

JOHN O'BRIEN SJ, born in Waterford on 20 December 1708, son of Thomas O'Brien and Mary Carroll, was received into the Society in 1725 and ordained in 1734. He took the oath on 17 March 1725 in Santiago. He was debited for supplies in college ledger, that is, books, ink and the hire of a mule from La Coruña. He received minor orders on 22 February 1725. Later he was rector in the Irish College, Salamanca. He was a fluent Irish speaker. He died in 1767.[250]

O COIN *see* Quinn

O'CONNELL *see* CONNELL

MAURICE O'CONNOR (his surname is given as Cornelio). He came to Santiago in 1644 with three other students. They paid 970 *reales* for their college expenses.[251]

O CONRY *see* CONROY

GODFREY O'DALY was from Brosna, Co. Kerry, son of Cowlimgulum O Daly and Syly Ing Daly (Sile Ingean Ni Dalaigh?). He studied philosophy in Santiago for three years under Fr Thomas Comerford SJ. He went on to Salamanca, aged 25 years, swore his oath in 1617 and received a BA in the university on 13 May 1617.[252]

MELCHOR O'DALY came to the college in Santiago in 1644 accompanied by three other students. They brought 970 *reales* to pay expenses.[253]

JOHN O'DEA came to Santiago in 1614 and paid 480 *reales*.[254]

---

247 Sal. Arch. 34/2, f. 10.　248 *Arch. Hib.* 4, p. 17; Sal. Arch. 34/2, f. 63. 249 Sal. Arch. 33/I/14.　250 Sal. Arch. XXIII/I/ii, XXIII/2 34/7; Couselo, op. cit., p. 24; Finnegan, op. cit., p. 128.　251 Sal. Arch. 34/2, f. 37.　252 *Arch. Hib.* 2, p. 34; 4, p. 12.　253 Sal. Arch. 34/2, f. 37.　254 Sal. Arch. 34/2. f. 10.

CORNELIUS O'DRISCOLL studied at the college before 1613. There is a Cornelius O'Driscoll who became a Benedictine, according to O'Sullivan Beare. There was also a Cornelius O'Driscoll on Sinnott's list. He made a declaration before the vicar general on 24 April 1613. He was aged 15 at that time.[255]

DANIEL O'DONNELL, son of the Lord of Baltimor. He appears on the list of O Sullivan Beare and he also made the declaration on 24 April 1613. He was 20 years old in 1613.[256]

DENIS O'DRISCOLL was a student of jurisprudence in the University of Santiago in 1613. He was notified that he was required to sign the declaration by the Provisor but I did not find his declaration.[257]

DERMISIO O'DRISCOLL was 20 years old in 1613 when he made his declaration before the *provisor*.[258]

THADY O'DRISCOLL was the eldest son of Dermisio O'Driscoll and is on O'Sullivan Beare's list. He was the son of the Lord of Castlehaven. There is a Tadgh O'Driscoll on Sinnott's list also but he does not identify him.[259]

O'HAIL *see* HALE

O'HELAN *see also* HELAN

JOHN O HELAN, son of Thady O Helan and Catalina O Duin, was from Queen's County (Laois). He was received in the college aged 26 years on 21 April 1659. He took an oath on 17 September 1659. He signed as Joannes Helanus or O Helan.[260]

O'HOULAGHAN *see* HOLLAND

OHUOLANUS *see* HOLLAND

O'KELLY *see* KELLY

O'LEA *see* LEE or LEA

JAMES O'MANNING (MANNIN) swore an oath on 17 March 1759 in Santiago and in Salamanca on 20 July 1760. He answered well for the first year examination on 8 October 1761 He left because of illness at the second year examination on 4 September. He received minor orders on 12 June

255 Sal. Arch. 33/I/15, 35/4.   256 Sal. Arch. 33/I/15.   257 Sal. Arch. 33/I/15, 35/4.   258 Sal. Arch. 33/I/15, 35/4.   259 Sal. Arch. 33/I/15, 35/4.   260 Sal. Arch. XXIII/I/i.

1760 in Santiago. The rector in Salamanca, Edward Lisvard, certified that this student had studied philosophy 'con mucho aprovechamiento' (with great benefit) in Santiago for three years and in Salamanca had studied scholastic, dogmatic and moral theology for one and a half years. He was an ordained priest and because of ill-health could not continue. The medical advice was that he should return to Ireland '*a tomar los aires naturales*' (to take the natural air there).[261]

EDMUND O'MEAGHER took the oath in Santiago on 17 March 1758 and in Salamanca on 20 July 1760. There are very good reports of his exams for first, second and third years in theology, he answered well, and 'very good' and 'excelled' were the words used. These examinations were on 8 October 1761, 4 September 1762 and 23 June 1763. He received minor orders on 12 June 1760 in Santiago.[262]

MALACHY O'MEAGHER (the name is given as Meachar) was a student in Santiago in 1614 from the diocese of Ossory. He received the degree of BA in the University of Salamanca on 13 May 1617. He was ordained in July 1619 and sent to Ireland.[263]

FELIX O'NEILL's main claim to fame was the prolonged investigation into his absences without leave from the college. He received and sent letters without permission and seemed to rebel against the strict rules of the seminary. He was in the college in 1631.[264]

OQUEN *see* QUINN

O QUIN *see* QUINN

O RIAN or O RYAN *see* RYAN

BUECIO (Boetius) O'SULLIVAN was 18 years old in 1613. He was then a student in the Irish College, Santiago de Compostela.[265]

DANIEL O'SULLIVAN was 20 years old in 1613, a student at the University of Santiago. He made a declaration in 1613.[266]

JAMES O'SULLIVAN was a student of Jurisprudence in University of Santiago *c.*1613. He may be the same as Buecio O'Sullivan above.[267]

---

261 Sal. Arch. I/2, XXIII/I/ii, XXIII/2; *Arch. Hib.* 4, pp 10, 41, 42.   **262** Sal. Arch. XXIII/I/ii, XXIII/2; *Arch. Hib.* 4, pp 10, 41, 42.   **263** Sal. Arch. 34/2, f. 10, 40/2; *Arch. Hib*, 3, p. 90; 4, p. 12.   **264** Sal. Arch. 33/1/15.   **265** Sal. Arch. 33/1/15, 35/4.   **266** Sal. Arch. 33/1/14 and 15, 35/4.   **267** Sal. Arch. 35/4.

PHILIP O'SULLIVAN, *maestro*, Master of Arts, of the University of Santiago, and a nephew of Donal O'Sullivan Beare. He is the famous historian. He was also a brother of Thadeus O Sullivan SJ, rector of the college (1629–31). He took the oath in Salamanca on 9 October 1620. He was born in Dursey Island, in the barony of Dunkerrin, diocese of Ardfert.[268]

THADY O'SULLIVAN (1) SJ, son of Dermot O'Sullivan and Cecily Carty, from Meen, Co. Kerry, diocese of Ardfert, studied philosophy at the Irish College of Santiago de Compostela. He was a brother of Philip O'Sullivan. He went on to the Irish College, Salamanca, aged 22 years, and took the oath there on 13 September 1618. He returned to Ireland in 1633 but was transported in Cromwellian times and returned to Spain, where he died in 1684.[269]

THADY O'SULLIVAN (2) paid 100 *reales* in 1657 in Santiago.[270]

THOMAS O'SULLIVAN went to Alcalá de Henares from Santiago in 1649 when that college was founded.[271]

THOMAS (HUMPHREY) O'SULLIVAN took the oath in Santiago on 18 March 1755, and in Salamanca on 8 September 1757. He was examined on 22 August 1758 and found 'satisfactory' He had received minor orders in Santiago on 17 June 1757. Couselo calls him Tomás Canturiense Humphirdo Sullivan. He left for Ireland from Bilbao on 25 June 1760.[272]

FRANCIS PHELAN swore the oath in Santiago on 18 March 1731 and in Salamanca on 18 May 1733. He received minor orders on 25 March 1733 from Bishop José Yermo de Santibáñez in his palace in Santiago. He was approved for first and second year theology on 29 July 1734 and 1735 and approved in both examination. He deposited 4 *doblones* in Santiago as shown in the ledger.[273]

---

268 Sal. Arch. 33/1/15, 35/4; *Arch. Hib.* 3, pp 91, 92. Philip O'Sullivan's work *Catholicii Iberniae Compendium* (Lisbon, 1621) on the history of the Nine Years War (1594–1603) is analysed by Clare Carroll in H. Morgan (ed.), *The battle of Kinsale* (Bray, 2004), pp 217–28. 269 *Arch. Hib.* 2, p. 35. See Finnegan, op. cit., pp 156–7. 270 Sal. Arch. 34/2, folio 57 v. 271 Arnáiz-Sancho, pp 61, 87–8. 272 Sal. Arch. I/3, XXIII/I/ii; *Arch. Hib.* 4, pp 9, 40; Couselo, op. cit., p. 25. He apparently used the name Humphrey in Santiago; cf. Ambhlaoibh Ó Súilleabháin, *Cín Lae Amhlaoibh*: this was obviously a family name in the O'Sullivan clan. 273 Sal. Arch. XXIII/I/ii, XXIII/2, 34/7; Couselo, op. cit., p. 24; *Arch. Hib.* 4, pp 6, 28, 29.

NICHOLAS PHELAN took the oath on 17 March 1752 in Santiago. He sat for the first examination in Salamanca on 26 August 1755 and did well. In the second year examination he was also approved on 22 August 1756. He left for Ireland on 26 June 1757.[274]

CHRISTOPHER PLUNKETT swore the oath on 8 October 1704 in Santiago.[275]

ROBERT PLUNKETT was 21 years old on 27 July 1631. He had been in the college in Santiago one year at that time. He came from Garristown in Ulster.[276]

PETER POWELL took the oath in Santiago on 17 March 1761 and in Salamanca on 16 July 1763. He was examined in first year on 25 August 1764 and in second year on 29 August 1765, and the verdict was that he answered 'middlingly'. In March 1765 he was ordained to the priesthood by the auxiliary bishop, Zelanese. He left for Ireland on 1 June 1766 with John Keaghry.[277]

JAMES POWER swore the oath in Santiago on 17 March 1764 and 24 March 1765.[278]

WILLIAM POWER. His oaths in Santiago are dated 17 March 1764, 1765 and 1766. He arrived in Salamanca on 11 June 1766 from Santiago. His oath is dated 22 June 1766. He finished his course and left for Ireland on 4 April 1770.[279]

JAMES PRENDERGAST paid a *limosna* of 220 *reales* in 1667 in Santiago.[280]

WALTER PRENDERGAST was a student in Santiago and paid 300 *reales* in 1623.[281]

JOHN PRONTY took the oath on 17 March 1728 in Santiago and went on to Salamanca, where he is recorded as being approved for the second year theology examination on 27 July 1729. He is noted as a 'choice student'. He was approved with a high encomium for his third year examnation on 31 August 1730. There is also extant a letter from him to the rector of Salamanca, John O'Brien, from Ballinenagh, Co. Cavan, Kilmore diocese, dated 4 December 1746.[282]

---

274 Sal. Arch. XXIII/I/ii; *Arch. Hib.* 4, pp 38, 39; Couselo, op. cit., p. 25. **275** Sal. Arch. XXIII/I/ii. **276** Sal. Arch. 33/1/15. **277** Sal. Arch. XXIII/I/ii; *Arch. Hib.* 4, pp 10, 43, 44. **278** Sal. Arch. XXIII/I/ii. **279** Sal. Arch. XXIII/I/ii; *Arch. Hib.* 4, pp 11, 45, 47. **280** Sal. Arch. 34/2, f. 72. **281** Sal. Arch. 34.2, f. 17. **282** Sal. Arch. XXIII/I/ii, 52/5/9; *Sal. Letters*, XVI/H/6/3, p. 284; *Arch. Hib.* 4, pp 26, 27.

HUGH PURCELL went from Santiago to Alcalá in 1649 when the Irish College was founded there.[283]

RICHARD PURFIELD was in the college in Santiago in 1699 and paid for maintenance. He received minor orders on 21 March 1703, sub-deaconship on 24 August, deaconship on 4 September 1703 and ordained to the priesthood on 17 March 1704, in Santiago, Bishop Monroy officiating. He was approved to pass into third year theology in Salamanca on 26 September 1705.[284]

ANDREW QUINN came from Santiago to Salamanca at the beginning of June 1649. He was from Co. Galway, diocese of Tuam. He took the oath in Salamanca on 8 October 1652. He was examined on 23 September 1650 and on 26 October 1651 and gave a good account of himself.[285]

BERNARD QUINN took oath in Santiago on 17 March 1752 and went on to Salamanca. He did well in his examinations in 1755 and 1756. He was ordained in 1755 by the bishop of Salamanca, don José Zorrilla, in St Martin's.[286]

EDMUND QUINN swore the oath in .Santiago on 17 March 1767 and moved to Salamanca in November 1769/. He left the seminary on 23 December 1769 as he had not a vocation.[287]

JOHN QUINN came to Santiago in 1644 with three other students. They brought 970 *reales* to pay to the college.[288]

PATRICK QUINN (1) took the oath in Salamanca on 28 May 1734, as Patrick Aloysius O Quinn. He took minor orders in Santiago on 25 March 1733 and had an account in the college ledger. He showed excellent ability at his first year examination in theology on 29 July 1735. At the second year examination in 1736 he also gave a very good account of himself.[289]

PATRICK QUINN (2) was presented for minor orders in Santiago by rector Araujo, document undated. He signed the oath on 12 September 1751 in Salamanca. At his first year examination on 26 August 1752 he answered well. Having been ordained he left for Ireland on 25 June 1753 in the

283 Arnáiz-Sancho, pp 61, 87–8. 284 Couselo, op. cit., p. 23; *Arch. Hib.* 4, p. 23; Sal. Arch. 34/2, f. 120. 285 *Arch. Hib.* 3, p. 107; 4, p. 15. 286 Sal. Arch. XXIII/I/ii; *Arch. Hib.* 4, p. 38; Couselo, op. cit., p. 25. 287 Sal. Arch. XXIII/I/ii; *Arch. Hib.* 4, pp 46, 47. 288 Sal. Arch. 34/2, f. 37. 289 Sal. Arch. 34/7; *Arch. Hib.* 4. pp 6, 29; Couselo, op. cit., p. 24.

company of Robert Stapleton. He left on the advice of the physicians as his health was bad.[290]

SILVESTER (O) QUINN swore an oath on 17 March 1741 in Santiago. He received minor orders on 9 April 1741. His oath in Salamanca is dated 16 May 1742. He also defended *Dominicales* in April 1744. His examinations took place on 29 August 1743 and 28 July 1744. He sought permission to stay in Salamanca for a fourth year but was turned down as the rules stated that students must leave after three years of theology. He answered very well at his examinations. He was ordained to the priesthood in March 1745 and left for Ireland before 25 June 1745.[291]

TERENCE QUINN took the oath on 17 March 1730 in Santiago where he received minor orders (*corona y grados*) in March 1733. He brought with him for deposit in Santiago *una moneda portuguesa y ocho de plata* (a Portuguese piece of money and a silver piece of eight). He arrived in Salamanca in 1733 and swore the oath there on 18 May. He was examined and approved for first year theology on 29 July 1734 and in second year on 29 July 1735.[292]

QUIERNANO *see* KIENAN

QUIRIBAM *see* KIRWAN

BARTHOLOMEW READ came to the college on 10 November 1639 and paid 700 *reales* together with William Kugancio.[293]

PETER READ (Redano) was a student in Santiago and paid 440 *reales* to the college in 1623 and in the same year a further 400 *reales*. He became a Jesuit in 1628 or 1629, was ordained 1633 or 1634 and was rector of the college in Santiago in 1647 until 1648. He was son of Peter Read and Alison Ward (Peart?), born Ratoath, Co. Meath, in 1606.[294]

PATRICK REDMOND took the oath in Santiago on 17 March 1734 and in Salamanca on 16 May 1736. He had received minor orders in Santiago on 20 October 1734. He came to the Irish College, Santiago de Compostela with John Codd on 22 October 1733 and brought 11 *doblones* to deposit in

---

290 Sal. Arch. XXIII/2, 34/7; *Arch. Hib.* 4, pp 8, 36. **291** Sal. Arch. I/3, XXIII/I/ii, XXIII/2; *Arch. Hib.* 4, pp 7, 29, 30, 31; Couselo, op. cit., p. 24. **292** Sal. Arch. XXIII/I/ii, 35/7; *Arch. Hib.* 4, pp 6, 28, 29; Couselo, op. cit., p. 24. **293** Sal. Arch. 34/2, f. 35. **294** Sal. Arch. 34/2, f. 17, 40/2; Finnegan, op. cit., p. 164. Cat. MSS. Hib. SJ, 1556–1669.

the college for the two of them. It is also noted that he and Codd were billed for mules to take them to Tuy for ordination, at a cost of 84 *reales* each. He was examined for first year theology on 4 August 1737 and for second year on 18 August 1738.[295]

PEDRO REVETO came to the college from Ireland in 1624 and paid 550 *reales*.[296]

PATRICK RICE (1) came to Salamanca from Santiago in 1680 in place of Joseph Walsh who had left for Ireland that year.[297]

PATRICK RICE (2) son of Nicholas Rice and Philida Vita (White?), from Munster. He was 25 years of age in 1655. He signed his oath in Santiago on 17 March 1655 as Patricius Riccius. The witnesses to his oath were James Joyce and Daniel Gaffney.[298]

RITE *see* WRIGHT

THOMAS ROCH(E) took the triple oath on 17 March 1713 in Santiago. He paid 356 *reales* and 489 *reales* as a boarder in the Irish College, Santiago sometime after 1713. On 9 September 1715 he signed the oath in Salamanca. He was from Wexford, diocese of Ferns. He was examined in the three theology courses on 28 September 1716 and answered well. He was one of the only two students in Salamanca at that time. On 28 September 1718 he was examined, gave a very good result and left that year for Ireland.[299]

PATRICK ROSSITER (1) entered Santiago as a student in 1657 with Edmund Stafford and they paid 170 *reales*. He was from Co. Wexford and was recommended by the bishop of Ferns.[300]

PATRICK ROSSITER (2) was son of William Rossiter and Elizabeth Roch from Co. Wexford, diocese of Ferns. He was aged 20 years on 22 September 1647 when he took the oath in Santiago. On 8 October 1650 he took the oath in Salamanca. He was examined early in June 1649 after his arrival from Santiago and approved. He was again examined on 23 September 1650 and gave a good account of himself. There is a letter written by him to Brother Staff on 2 May 1701.[301]

295 Sal. Arch. XXIII/I/ii, XXIII/2, 34/7; *Arch. Hib.* 4, pp 7, 29; Finnegan, op. cit., p. 164.   296 Sal. Arch. 34/2, f. 18.   297 *Arch. Hib.* 4, p. 20.   298 Sal. Arch. XXIII/I/i. 299 Sal. Arch. XXIII/I/ii, 34/2, f. 135 v.140, 143v; *Arch. Hib.* 4, pp 5, 24.   300 Sal. Arch. 34/2, f. 57 v.   301 Sal. Arch. XXIII/I/i; *Arch. Hib.* 3, p. 107; 4, p. 15; *Sal.*

JEREMIAH RYAN took oath on 17 March 1734 (or 1732) in Santiago. He received minor orders on 25 March 1733. He had a ledger account in Santiago. He took the oath in Salamanca on 28 May 1734. He was examined in first year 29 July 1735 and approved. He gave a good account in his examination for second year on 29 July 1736.[302]

THADY RYAN paid 300 *reales* in Santiago in *c.*1675. His oath in Salamanca is dated 10 September 1677.[303]

THOMAS RYAN received minor orders in Santiago in *c.*1747, from Antonio Riomol, bishop of Mondoñado, with permission of the ordinary.[304]

JOHN ST JOHN took oath on 17 March 1740 in Santiago and on 16 May 1742 in Salamanca. According to ledger he borrowed small amounts from time to time. He was presented for minor orders by rector Araujo in Santiago, no date given.[305]

WALTER SALINGER paid 100 *reales* for board in 1657 in Santiago.[306]

EDWARD SALUS was a witness for Patrick Everard on 2 May 1670, in Santiago. He came to Salamanca on 14 October 1673 and took an oath there on 17 March 1674 that he would offer masses for the rector's intentions. He was examined for second year theology on 1 October 1674.[307]

ANDREW SAUL entered Santiago on 10 February 1640 and gave 160 *reales* to the college. The were two Andrew Sauls, one became an apostate.[308]

IGNATIUS SAUL was presented for minor orders in Santiago on 16 December 1650 by rector Lombard. He was from the archdiocese of Cashel. He took the oath in Salamanca on 8 December 1652.[309]

JOHN SHAUGNESSY came to Salamanca from Santiago in May 1664 where he had been examined and approved before leaving.[310]

EDMUNDO SHEA was in the college from October 1731 to October 1734.[311]

Letters 13 AA 1 10; this may be Nicholas Stafford, which we see in Chapter 6. **302** Sal. Arch. XXIII/I/ii, 34/7; *Arch. Hib.* 4, pp 7, 29; Couselo, op. cit., p. 24. **303** Sal. Arch. 34/2, f. 80; *Arch. Hib.* 3, pp 111. **304** Couselo, op. cit., p. 25. **305** Sal. Arch. XXIII/I/ii, XXIII/2, 34/7; *Arch. Hib.* 4, p. 7. **306** Sal. Arch. 34/2, f. 57. **307** Sal. Arch. XXIII/I/i; *Arch. Hib.* 3, pp 110, 111; 4, p. 19. **308** Sal. Arch. 34/2, f. 35. Is he Andrew Fitzbennett, Finnegan, op. cit., pp 172/3? The two Andrew Sauls were cousins, one apostatised in 1682, one was rector of the Irish College, Salamanca. **309** Sal. Arch. XXIII/2; *Arch. Hib.* 3, p. 107. **310** *Arch. Hib.* 4, p. 17. **311** Sal. Arch. 34/7.

JOHN SHEA took the oath in Santiago on 17 March 1749.[312]

SIMON SHEA SJ, swore the oath on 17 March 1725 in Santiago. He had a ledger account in the college. He took minor orders on 24 February 1725. He is also listed as Simon Shill. He was a nephew of Patrick Shee, bishop of Ossory, born in Kilkenny on 28 March 1706; entered the Society in Seville 28 January 1726. He died on 16 May 1773.[313]

WILLIAM SHEA was a student in Santiago and paid 440 *reales* to the college in 1623. A William Shea from Kilkenny became an Augustinian in 1629, according to Salamanca records.[314]

MORGANUS SHEEHY took the oath on 21 September 1631 in Santiago. He was questioned during the Felix O'Neill investigation.[315]

NICHOLAS SHEEHY took the oath in Santiago on 17 March 1746 and received minor orders from bishop Taboada in Santiago on 14 November 1747. He took the oath in Salamanca on 17 March 1749, defended *Dominicales* and did very well at the first year examination in 1749. He was expelled on 18 March or 18 May 1751. He was the ring-leader in the unfortunate incident of the break-down in discipline in the college in Salamanca referred to as the Sheehy episode.[316]

ANTHONY SHERLOCK paid 198 *reales* in 1662 for his outfit in Santiago and 160 *reales* in 1664. He paid in *pesos* in 1663.[317]

PAUL SHERLOCK came to the college in 1624 from Ireland and paid 80 *reales*.[318]

SHILL (SHEIL) *see* SHEA.

RICHARD (JOHN) SINNOTT (1) was in the college at the time of the takeover and presented himself for the declaration. He is the brother of Patrick Sinnott who wrote the report in favour of the Jesuit takeover of the college in 1613.[319]

RICHARD SINNOTT (2) took the oath on 17 March 1730 in Santiago.[320]

---

312 Sal. Arch. XXIII/I/ii.   **313** Sal. Arch. XXIII/I/ii; Couselo, op. cit., p. 24; Finnegan, op. cit., p. 179.   **314** Sal. Arch. 34/2, f. 17, 40/2.   **315** Sal. Arch. XXIII/I/i, 33/1/15, 34/7.   **316** Sal. Arch. XXIII/I/ii, 33/I/15, 34/4; *Arch. Hib.* 4, pp 8, 34; Couselo, op. cit., p. 25. See Chapter 6 for details of the Sheehy episode. **317** Sal. Arch. XIII, 34/2, ff 65, 67, 52/2. The *peso* was another old coin, worth about 576 *maravedis* in 1609.   **318** Sal. Arch. 34/2, f. 18. See Chapter 4 on rectors. **319** Sal. Arch. 33/1/15, 35/4.   **320** Sal. Arch. XXIII/I/ii.

MICHAEL SMITH swore oath on 17 March 1740 in Santiago and in Salamanca on 16 May 1742. He was from diocese of Kilmore. He was debited 19 *reales* for a waistcoat in 1740 in the college ledger in Santiago. He did well in his first year examination in Salamanca on 29 August 1743 and very well in his examination for second year theology on 28 July 1744. He left for the mission on 25 June 1745.[321]

EDMUND STAFFORD, son of Nicholas Stafford and Maria Barnwell from Co. Wexford, was aged 21 years when he took the oath on 17 August 1658 in Santiago. He came with Patrick Rossiter (1) and they paid a joint amount of 170 *reales* on entering the college. He was presented for minor orders by rector Salinger in Santiago on 16 September 1660.[322]

GASPAR STAFFORD SJ took the oath in Santiago on 17 March 1718 and in Salamanca 4 September 1721. He was son of James Stafford and Maria Deveroux of Wexford, was born 10 May 1698, entered the Society on 17 October 1723. At his examinations on 24 September 1722 and 24 September 1723 he was judged to have extraordinary talent. He was rector in Salamanca from 1730 to 1743.[323]

JOHN STAFFORD (1) was presented for minor orders in Santiago on 21 September 1708.[324]

JOHN STAFFORD (2) took minor orders in Santiago on 17 June 1757, Bishop Bartolome Rajoy officiating. His oath in Salamanca is dated 8 September 1757. On 22 August 1758 and 30 August 1759 he was examined and found satisfactory but in his third year on 23 June 1760 he showed want of study. He left via Bilbao for Ireland on 26 June 1760.[325]

NICHOLAS STAFFORD SJ: see Chapter 7 for a note on this student.

EDWARD SWEETMAN was 24 years old in 1613 and was a student in the Irish College, Santiago at that time.[326]

NICHOLAS SWEETMAN took the oath on 17 March 1719. His Salamanca oath is dated 4 September 1721. He went on the mission in 1724. He became bishop of Ferns (1745–86) and was exiled. He was auxiliary to the

---

321 Sal. Arch. I/3, XXIII/I/ii, 34/7, 52/5/9; *Arch. Hib.* 4, pp 7, 29, 30, 31.   322 Sal. Arch. XXIII/I/i, XXIII/2, 34/2. f. 57 v.   323 Sal. Arch. XXIII/I/ii; *Arch. Hib.* 4, p. 1; 5, 2; Finnegan, op. cit., p. 184.   324 Couselo, op. cit., p. 23.   325 Sal. Arch. I/3; Couselo, op. cit., p. 25; *Arch. Hib.* 4, pp 9, 40.   326 Sal. Arch. 35/4.

bishop of Santiago. There is a letter from him, 30 August 1753, to Michael Fitzgerald, Wexford.[327]

PETER TAFFE; his Santiago oath is dated 15 August 1648 and his Salamanca oath 9 October 1650. He was from Co. Louth. He was examined in June 1649 and on 23 September 1650. On 31 May 1650 he signed oath testifying that he had said all masses he was bound to say.[328]

NICHOLAS TEELING came to Salamanca as a licentiate from Santiago on 22 September 1667 and was examined and signed the oath there on 6 October 1667.[329]

JOHN TIERNAN arrived in Salamanca from Santiago on October 1679 having been examined and approved in Santiago.[330]

RICHARD TOBIN was from from Corbally, diocese of Limerick, the son of Richard Tobin and Elisam Gibbons. He studied philosophy in Compostela from c.1614 to 1617 under Fr Thomas Comerford SJ before going to Salamanca. He was aged 21 years on 10 March 1617. He received a BA on 13 May 1617 in the University of Salamanca.[331]

JOHN TULLEN studied Arts in Santiago and then went on to Salamanca. He later left Salamanca in June 1763 to become a cadet in the Regimiento de Hibernia.[332]

LORENZO ROBERT TYRO paid 400 *reales* in Santiago on 7 December 1617.[333]

ROBERT JACOBUS TYWAE (Tighe?) is Jacobus, James, in later records. He was from Kilkenny, diocese of Ossory, father Nicholas and mother Katherine Bren. He enrolled in Salamanca aged 19 years and took the oath there on 16 December 1613. He was sent to Santiago to follow the three courses in philosophy and then returned to Salamanca and on 17 March 1617 he took the oath there. He was ordained on 14 April, completed his studies and was sent to Ireland in 1621. He is the first student I found who was sent from Salamanca to Santiago to study philosophy for three years.[334]

---

327 Sal. Arch. XXIII/I/ii, 52/5/121; *Arch. Hib.* 3, p. 113; 4, pp 5, 25.   328 Sal. Arch. XXIII/I/i; *Arch. Hib.* 3, pp 103, 104; 4, p. 15.   329 *Arch. Hib.* 3, p. 108; 4, p. 18. 330 *Arch. Hib.* 4, p. 20.   331 *Arch. Hib.* 2, p. 33; 4, p. 12.   332 *Arch. Hib.* 4 (1915), p. 43.   333 Sal. Arch. 34/2, f. 11.   334 *Arch. Hib.* 2, p. 29; 4, p. 12.

VADIM *see* WADDING

JAMES PAUL WADDING arrived in Salamanca in October 1679 from Santiago where he had been examined and was approved. Paulo Vadim was in Santiago in 1673 in November 1673 and paid 260 *reales*. I am presuming that this man is the same as James Paul Wadding.[335]

WALLSON *see* WATSON

CHRISTOPHER WALSH was in Santiago in 1664 and paid with his brother, James, 640 *reales*. He and his brother arrived from Santiago as licentiates to Salamanca on 22 September 1667. He and his brother signed the oath there on 6 October 1667.[336]

JAMES WALSH? was in Santiago with his brother Christopher in 1664. He went from Santiago as a licentiate to Salamanca on on 22 September 1667. He stayed on for a further year of theology and was examined in 1670.[337]

JOHN WALSH SJ (Valois) paid a *limosna* in Santiago in 1667 for 185 *reales*. He came from Santiago de Compostela to Salamanca in October 1670 and was approved. He signed an oath there in October or November 1671. He was son of Patrick Walsh and Isabel Russell, born in Co. Dublin on 19 March 1636, entered the Society in 1671. He was rector of Salamanca, 1686–92. He died in Bilbao on 2 January 1695.[338]

JOSEPH WALSH was in Santiago in 1672 where he paid 500 *reales* for his keep some months before the start of the course. He went from Santiago to Salamanca in October 1676. He swore an oath on 19 October 1677. He was kept on for a fourth year in 1679. He left for Ireland in 1680.[339]

PETER WALSH took oath on 17 March 1758 in Santiago and in Salamanca on 20 July 1760. He was ordained in Alba de Tormes on 28 December 1760 and had received minor orders in Santiago on 12 June 1760. His examinations were for first year on 8 October 1761 and for second on 4 September 1762. He left for home on 10 May 1763.[340]

---

335 *Arch. Hib.* 4, p. 20; Sal. Arch. 34/2, f. 80.   336 *Arch. Hib.* 3, p. 108; 4, p. 18; Sal. Arch. 34/2, f. 67.   337 *Arch. Hib.* 4, p. 18; Sal. Arch. 34/2, ff 67.   338 *Arch. Hib.* 3, p. 108; 4, p. 18; Sal. Arch. 34/2, f. 72.   339 *Arch. Hib.* 3, p. 111; 4, pp 19, 20; Sal. Arch. 34/2, f. 79 v.   340 Sal. Arch. XXIII/I/ii, XXIII/2; *Arch. Hib.* 4, pp 10, 41, 42.

JOHN WARD swore the oath on 17 March 1725 in Santiago. He was presented for minor orders in Santiago on 24 February 1725. He is debited for clothing in the ledger. He was born Dublin, 2 February 1704, entered the Society on 28 October 1725, ordained sever years later. He was called to Ireland in 1738 and was stationed in Dublin. He died there on 12 October 1775.[341]

ANDREW WATSON (WALLSON) arrived from Santiago in Salamanca on 19 September 1709. He had been approved in philosophy there. He was examined in Salamanca on 28 September 1710 and approved for second year. He gave a very good account at his third year exam on 28 September 1711. He left for Ireland in 1712.[342]

GASPAR WHITE took the oath in Santiago on 14 June 1656. He was examined and approved in Salamanca on 6 October 1657.[343]

GERALD or GERARD WHITE was presented for minor orders in Santiago on 16 December 1650? and on 9 December 1652 took the oath in Salamanca. He was from Westmeath. He was ordained by the bishop of Avila on 29 October 1652.

JAMES WHITE (1) took the oath in Santiago on 17 March 1714. He was presented for minor orders in Santiago (no date) He came to Salamanca on 6 September 1715. He took the triple oath on 4 October 1715 in Salamanca.[345]

JAMES WHITE (2) arrived in Salamanca on 2 July 1733 from Santiago and approved for theology. He was examined for second year on 29 July 1735 and it was stated that he was of excellent ability. He took the oath in Santiago on 17 March 1731 and in Salamanca on 18 May 1733. He was ordained (minor order) in Santiago on 25 March 1733.[346]

JAMES WHITE (3) arrived in Salamanca in October 1679 from Santiago, where he had been examined and approved.[347]

JOHN (MICHAEL) WHITE SJ was from a Meath family, was possibly reared in Dublin. He came to Salamanca from Santiago in July 1745. He took the

341 Sal. Arch. XXIII/I/ii, XXIII/2, 34/7.   342 *Arch. Hib.* 4, pp 23, 24; Sal. Arch. I/3.   343 Sal. Arch. XXIII/I/i; *Arch. Hib.* 4, p. 16.   344 Sal. Arch. I/3, XXIII/2; *Arch. Hib.* 3, p. 107.   345 Sal. Arch. XXIII/2, XXIII/I/ii; *Arch. Hib.* 4, p. 5.   346 Sal. Arch. XXIII/I/ii; *Arch. Hib.* 4, pp 6, 28, 29; Couselo, op. cit., p. 24.   347 *Arch. Hib,* 4, p. 20.

oath on 17 March 1743 in Santiago and in Salamanca on 31 July 1745. He was received into the Jesuits on 23 March 1746 in Villagarcia and was ordained on 21 September 1751. He returned to Ireland in failing health and died in Dublin on 14 February 1755.[348]

JOHN NICHOLAS WHITE paid 400 *reales* in Santiago on 7 December 1617.[349]

MARTIN WHITE was presented for minor orders on 16 December 1650 by rector Lombard in Santiago. Born Waterford 11 November 1637, entered the Society 7 November 1651, ordained 1661. He was a naval chaplain. He returned to Ireland 1670/1 and worked in Waterford until his death on 8 June 1693.[350]

MICHAEL THOMAS WHITE paid 360 *reales* in Santiago on 7 December 1617.[351]

NICHOLAS WHITE, from the diocese of Dublin, swore the oath in Santiago on 17 March 1746, and was ordained in minor orders on 14 November 1747 by Bishop Gil Taboada. He took the oath in Salamanca on 17 March 1749, and was examined there on 26 August 1749 and approved. He did very well in his examinations. He was expelled on 31 August 1750 as a result of the Sheehy affair. His letter in 1753 to John O'Brien show him to be in very low spirits.[352]

PATRICK WHITE (1) came to Santiago with three other students in 1641, bringing 970 *reales* to college coffers. They were Maurice O'Connor, John Quinn and Melchor Daly.[353]

PATRICK WHITE (2) took the oath in Santiago on 17 March 1702 where he studied arts and was ordained to minor orders in June 1703 and was ordained to the priesthood on 26 June 1707. The rector applied for his viaticum to return home.[354]

PETER WHITE SJ, born in Waterford, nephew of Thomas White, entered the novitiate at Seville sometime between 1619 and 1622. Prior to that he

---

348 Sal. Arch. XXIII/I/ii; *Arch. Hib.* 4, pp 7, 31; Finnegan, op. cit., p. 208; see *Sal. Letters* 13 AA 1 97, p. 11 for a letter to John O'Brien, rector Salamanca, from John Michael White in 1750. **349** Sal. Arch. 34/2, f. 11. **350** Sal. Arch. XXIII/2; Finnegan, op. cit., p. 208. **351** Sal. Arch. 34/2, f. 11. **352** Sal. Arch. XXIII/I/ii, 52/5/2–16; *Arch. Hib.* 4, pp 8, 34; Couselo, p. 25. **353** Sal. Arch. 34/2, f. 37. **354** Sal. Arch. I/3, XXIII/I/ii; Couselo, p. 23.

had been a student of Arts at the Irish College in Santiago. There was a Peter White in the Irish College, Santiago around the year 1623 when he paid 205 *reales*. He was rector in Seville from 27 February 1647 to 1650 and from 7 December 1656 and 7 September 1666. He was procurator of the Irish Colleges from 1639 to 1646. He died in 1678.[355]

RICHARD WHITE took the oath on 17 March 1706 in Santiago.[356]

PATRICK WRIGHT, who appears as Rite, paid 300 *reales* for outfitting in 1676.[357]

355 Sal. Arch. 34/2, f. 17. See Finnegan, *IER*, 1966, pp 46, 55–6.   356 Sal. Arch. XXIII/I/ii.   357 Sal. Arch. 34/2, f. 84 v.

CHAPTER 6

Persons and Events

After the death of Philip II in 1598 things went horribly wrong for Ireland. The Spanish had been engaged in a long and costly conflict with England. They had suffered two major defeats (the Armada and Kinsale), were being harassed by the Dutch rebels in the Low Countries and were under duress also on the high seas and in the New World. Before the king's death it was clear that Spain was on the brink of bankrupcy after the disaster of the Armada. This combined with the debacle in Kinsale made it inevitable for the kingdom to make peace with England. After long negotiations a treaty was signed in 1604 between the two kingdoms.[1]

In this delicate situation Spain could not be seen to harbour the enemies of England, and when Donal O'Sullivan Beare, who had been a staunch adherent of the Spanish monarch Philip II during the Nine Years War (1594–1603), arrived in Spain in 1604 to escape inevitable imprisonment and death in the Tower of London, the situation became tense. He had lost everything by throwing in his lot with the Spanish at Kinsale and at Dunboy after the defeat at Kinsale. He was not pardoned for his part in the struggle. (O'Neill and O'Donnell were, but the 'pardon' was short-lived.) When he came to Spain he was received by the Conde de Caracena, Luís de Carillo, governor of Galicia from 1596 until 1606, in the name of Philip III. The count was a friend of long-standing of O'Sullivan, whose elder son, Daniel, had been brought up in his household.[2]

---

1 This was the Treaty of London, August 1604. See Morgan (ed.), *The battle of Kinsale*, p. 227, for an interesting portrait of the negotiators by Juan Pantoja de da Cruz from the National Portrait Gallery, London. See Ann Chambers, *At arm's length* (Dublin, 2004), pp 21–37 for a very good summing-up of the pre-Kinsale period in Ireland.   2 Luís de Carillo, Conde de Caracena, was the friend and benefactor of the Irish in Galicia. Daniel O'Sullivan, elder son of Donal Cam, became a page at court in 1606 and in 1607 a knight of Santiago. He was killed in an accident in the palace in Madrid in 1610: see Micheline Kerney Walsh, 'O Sullivan Beare in Spain: some unpublished documents', *Arch. Hib.* (1990), p. 47 and *Knights,* i, p. 1. See also Ciaran O'Scea, 'Caracena: champion of the Irish, hunter of the Moriscos' in Morgan (ed.), *The battle of Kinsale*, pp 229–39.

On the eve of the treaty with England, O'Sullivan and his followers were on the king's doorstep in Galicia. That is where they were kept, or else they were encouraged to go to the Low Countries where several Irish regiments were based. Even in 1607 the great Hugh O'Neill, when he had taken flight from Ireland for the same reasons as O'Sullivan Beare, was prevented from coming to Spain and was prevailed upon to go to Rome instead. The flight of O'Neill, O'Donnell, O'Sullivan Beare and many other Irish aristocrats and leaders abroad occurred at the time due to the widespread executions in the Tower and in Ireland; dispossession and disenfranchisement became the order of the day, and the people were left leaderless and broken in spirit. The plantation of Ulster in 1610, Oliver Cromwell's ruthless campaigns in Ireland, the defeat at the Boyne, the broken Treaty of Limerick, Aughrim – the list goes on and on – all combined to make the seventeenth century the final disaster for Ireland.

The college in Santiago de Compostela was endowed by Philip III in 1605 with an annual grant, and it was left to the Irish, or the followers of O'Sullivan, to run it themselves. Ostensibly, it was to carry out the education of the sons of the followers of Donal Cam. Irish Colleges for the education of secular priests had been established in the Iberian peninsula before Santiago de Compostela, in Lisbon in 1590 and in Salamanca in 1592. Both these colleges were administered by Irish Jesuits. The colleges thus founded were not the property of the Society of Jesus and, in general, were set up by the reigning monarch and funded by the kingdom. The college in Santiago had functioned under these conditions until 1613 when the king ordered that the rector of the college be dismissed and the institution handed over to the governance of the Jesuits.

The year 1613 was then a defining point for the Irish College in Santiago de Compostela. The transfer of the running of the college to the Jesuits had far-reaching effects and was a turning point in the position of the Irish in Spain. They were now clearly divided into Old-Irish and Old-English. The latter, although adhering to the old faith, had different attitudes and loyalties vis-à-vis the English monarchy to the Gaelic Irish. The Jesuits were favoured by the Spanish monarch at the time as the great educators and as being in the vanguard of the forces ranged against the Lutherans. Many of the Irish Jesuits were of English extraction; many came from the English towns in Munster and along the south coast of Leinster, as well as from other parts of the Pale. While faithful to the Catholic faith, they were perceived in Old Irish or Gaelic circles as loyal, or at least ambiguous in their loyalty, to the English crown in Ireland.

Needless to say, many of the Irish Jesuits could not be described thus, and many were, in fact, Irish-speaking as well.

The followers of O'Sullivan Beare and others saw the handover of the Irish College in Santiago to the Irish Jesuits as a betrayal. They had lost all in their efforts in Kinsale to rid Ireland of the English domination. In his memorial Fr Eugene MacCarthy, the ousted rector of the Irish College, goes even so far as to accuse some of the Old English, whose sons were clerical students in the Irish College at Salamanca, of having fought against the Spanish at Kinsale.

It is difficult to isolate the reasons for the handing over of the college to the Jesuits. There were undoubtedly complaints and rumblings of dissatisfaction with the running of the college. However, the most serious factor was that the students were not required to take an oath in Santiago at that time as in the other Irish and English Colleges in Spain pledging to return to Ireland and England after ordination. A document was submitted to the Consejo de Estado (Council of State), signed by six members on 9 March 1613, stating that they understood that the college was conducted with great disorder, that the archbishop of Santiago, having been asked for his opinion in a letter of 10 February 1613, agreed with the six councillors and that he indicated that the Irish priest who administered the college, while a worthy man, was not suitable for the job.[3]

The granting of a special faculty to any rector of a continental Irish College to present seminarians for ordination, which was normally the function of bishops, was the kernel of the matter. A special papal faculty had been granted to the rector of a continental Irish College to propose clerical students for ordination. In the emergency conditions then prevailing in Ireland, with most of the prelates exiled or in hiding this was deemed essential. However, papal blessing was given on the condition that the oath was administered to all collegians. That this was not being carried out in Santiago may have prompted the archbishop of Cashel, David Kearney, to prevail on the king, through the intermediary of the Spanish ambassador in London in 1612, to hand over the running of the college to the Jesuits.

The then-rector, Eugene MacCarthy, made a strong protest against the proposed takeover.[4] The main points from his memo were that he had

3 Jesuit Archives ICOL/SANT/1 (Legajo 2643, Archivo General de Simancas); Sal. Arch. 33/1/15. 4 See Gareth A. Davies, 'The Irish College at Santiago de Compostela: two documents about its early days' in Margaret Rees et al. (eds),

been under the impressions that the Jesuits had given up troubling the college, but he now heard from court that they were slandering the members of the college and trying to get them thrown out of it. The attacks of the Jesuits (he said) were due to ambition and self-interest, just as it was in France where they tried to oust Fr Dermot MacCarthy, a priest of good life and nephew (he was, in fact, the son) of a titled gentleman, Sir Cormac MacCarthy,[5] who was responsible for the setting up of colleges in Bordeaux, Toulouse, Aix and Cahors which had sent out seventeen ordained priest to their afflicted country. He accused the Jesuit order of losing a college at Valladolid, and of attempts to take over one in Seville. He asserted that the Jesuits in the Salamanca college were not Irish but English and claimed that nineteen persons whose sons were in the Irish College there helped the English at Kinsale and opposed the Spaniards. On the other hand, all those who were in the Irish College, Santiago sided with the Spaniards and the Catholic cause. If the take-over proceeds in Santiago they will oust the *real* Irish who wish to instruct the faithful in the true faith all over Ireland not just in the cities which are populated with merchants and artisans descended from Englishmen and whose sons studying for the priesthood are unable to keep the Irish in the faith because they do not know the Irish language and are naturally inclined towards the English. They are only, therefore, of use as priests in places where English is spoken. This information, he says, is not known to His Majesty. The letter is signed 22 April 1612 by Eugene MacCarthy.

There is some truth in MacCarthy's belief that the Irish language was neglected by the Jesuits from the Pale. The early Jesuits in Ireland mostly belonged to the Old English families. There were, of course, notable exceptions. The majority of the Jesuits who ran the college initially would have been English-speaking from southern royalist towns, such as Waterford, Wexford, Cashel, Clonmel, and possibly some blame for the abandonment of Irish could be laid at their door. Irish did become an issue from time to time in the colleges, but clearly the death knell of the language dated from this period. English became the predominant language in the continental colleges and in the cities in Ireland.[6]

Catholic tastes and times; essays in honour of M.E. Williams (Leeds, 1987) pp 108–9. For the complete text of MacCarthy's protest memorial see Sal. Arch. 33/1/15 **5** T.J. Walsh, op. cit., p. 88. He was Sir Callaghan MacTeige MacCarthy. **6** See T.J.Walsh, op. cit. on the Irish language in the Irish Colleges, pp 150, 158–61.

The Irish Jesuits had some part in the initial proposal for the take-over of the college and actively supported it. It was also supported by an Irish academic, Patrick Sinnott, resident in Santiago, who earlier had been tutor to the children of the Conde de Caracena and who went on to a distinguished, if turbulent, career in the University of Santiago. He wrote a strongly worded memorial to the authorities, pointing out what he perceived to be the faults of the college, up to that time.[7] The division is clearly seen in the adherents to both sides in the struggle for and against the take-over.

Ofelia Rey Castelao tells us that Patrick Sinnott arrived in Galicia in the 1580s with his parents, who had to leave Ireland because of religious persecution. He competed unsuccessfully for a chair in the University of Santiago in 1602. He appears to have been an adviser on Irish matters to the governor of Galicia. He spent some time in Noia as a private teacher until eventually in 1611, after a somewhat turbulent competition, he secured a university chair. His career was extremely controversial and troubled and included clashes with the Inquisition. He ended up in prison, was accused of being an *astrólogo judiciario* (a judicial astrologer), dipping into the books of the *grandes nigromantes* (the great necromancers) and practising fortunetelling by observation of the planets and so forth.[8]

Grouped on the other side of the deep divide were the great Franciscan archbishop of Tuam, Florence Conry, always a defender of Gaelic interests in Spain and a close friend and advisor of Hugh O'Neill, and, naturally enough, Donal O'Sullivan and his numerous followers in Spain. O'Sullivan firmly believed that the college had been set up originally as a secular college with a Catholic ethos for the education of the sons of his followers who had accompanied him into exile in Spain. It had been for them like a university residence but quite definitely not a seminary. There were numerous memorials from all the protagonists, but the main one emanated from Donal Cam O'Sullivan himself. It was promptly answered anonymously, point by point, paragraph by paragraph, by the Irish Jesuits in 1617. O'Sullivan's memorial setting out his twenty-eight arguments is not dated but was composed sometime before the Jesuit answer to it in

7 See Patricia O Connell, 'The Irish College, Santiago de Compostela 1605–1767', *Arch. Hib.*, 50 (1996), where his memorial is quoted in full, with English translation, pp 20–2. Sal. Arch. 33/1/15. **8** See 'Exiliados irlandeses en Santiago de Compostela desde fines del XVI a mediados del XVII', op. cit., pp 99–100. Luis Seoana, an exiled Galician writer living in Argentina, wrote in 1959 a drama

1617. So it would appear the dispute had dragged on even after the Jesuits had taken over control of the college.[9]

The author of the detailed answer to the memorial was thought to have been either Fr William White SJ or Fr Richard White SJ, but opinion now generally favours Fr Richard Conway SJ, who became the first Jesuit rector of the college at the take-over.[10]

So the first event of significance in the life of the college was the transfer of control of it to the Jesuits in April 1613. There was lasting bitterness about the change, and O'Sullivan never gave up hope that the decision would be reversed in time. After the demise of Philip II and the murder of O'Sullivan Beare in 1618, Spanish armed support for the Irish aspiration to rid Ireland of English rule was a non-starter. The Irish in Spain became completely integrated into Spanish life and they ceased to believe in ever returning to their homeland. Many rose to great heights in Spanish life. They were welcomed into the nobility and given the highest honours.[11] But there was no further 'Spanish ale' for Dark Rosaleen, and the exiles finally realised that fact. Spain did, however, continue to support the education of Irish seminarians for the priesthood, and this remained Ireland's main contact with their old ally through the dark and terrible centuries that followed.

The letter of the Duque de Lerma, dated 1 April 1613, to the provincial of the Jesuits in Castille, Pedro Maldonado, had an almost immediate result in the college and set the process in motion.[12] The students in the Irish College were ordered forthwith to appear before the provisor (vicar general) of the archdiocese of Santiago, don Diego de la Hoz. The duke had indicated to the provincial that a declaration was to be taken from each student on oath that he would comply with the order of His Majesty and subject himself to the rules and conditions prevailing in the other Irish and English seminaries in Spain. The students were summoned to appear at an *auto* (tribunal) to state if they would comply with His Majesty's order; in other words, Were they prepared to take an oath to become priests at the end of their course and return to Ireland to preach the gospel? They were asked to reply on oath 'yes' or 'no' to set questions. It is

El irlandés astrólogo, about this complex sixteenth-century scholar. **9** Sal. Arch. 33/1/15. **10** Davies, op. cit., p. 92. **11** Micheline Kerney Walsh's series *Spanish knights of Irish origin* is clearly a testimonial to the many who were raised to the highest honours in Spanish life and joined the ranks of the Knights of Santiago, Calatrava and Alcántara. **12** Sal. Arch. 33/1/14/15.

obvious that they believed that the whole business was a Jesuit plot and they had decided on concerted action, that is, to refuse to take the oath even though many of them wished to become priests. The students were duly notified on 24 April by writ and agreed to appear.[13]

Their reasons for declining to take the oath were strongly put by their main spokesman, Philip O'Sullivan, nephew of Donal Cam. He points out that the first royal decree of His Majesty by which he graciously gave support to the college ordered only that the students should be educated in virtue and good letters. He says the Society of Jesus may have a new *cédula* or decree from the king but that he and the other students have not seen it. They are all sons of persons who lost everything by going to the defence of the Catholic cause and his royal property and forces when his general don Juan del Aguila was in the kingdom of Ireland. The students in the college made statements in the same vein but on principle refused to sign the oath that they would become priests. They were promptly expelled and the take-over was accomplished almost overnight. In fact, the Jesuit fathers took over the college on Friday 26 April and the students were dismissed on the following Monday, 29 April 1613.

Donal Cam himself points out that most of the students since the foundation of the college had of their own volition in after years become priests. He goes on to claim that many persons of great sufficiency and letters had come out of the college and, further, that since disorders, commotions and indecencies are quite common in the university, Our Lord has freed and guarded 'these our students from all vices and they have emerged with singular purity and honour for the nine years that they have lived in Santiago without any occasion of scandal, with sobriety in their conduct'.

He agrees that they have no constitution in the college and have not had one from the beginning – only the house rules 'to live well and virtuously' which means two rosaries every day, litanies, psalms and other prayers for His Catholic Majesty, his kingdom and states, the propagation of the faith and for all their benefactors, receiving confession and communion every fortnight, living in peace, harmony and love and going out together to attend their studies.

They do not swear to become priests nor does His Majesty oblige them to since they are sons of noblemen delivered as hostages to the loyalty their parents have sworn to His Majesty. Further, that while Ireland needs

13 Ibid.

priests she also needs gentlemen brought up in the Catholic faith to receive and shelter them when the priests set foot back in Ireland. They also need scholars, principally canonists, to settle ecclesiastical cases. These are truly in short supply since the king of England does not permit study or schools except those which teach heresy.

The names of the students are given in the opening paragraphs of Chapter 5. In addition, Thady Driscoll, son of Dionisio, was nominated as interpreter at the *auto*. Eleven witnesses were also appointed, these were: Dionisio Driscol, Dermicio Conrrio, Thady O'Sullivan, Dermecio O Driscol, Thady Carty, Dermicio Carty, Dermicio O'Sullivan, Cornelio O'Driscoll, Bernardo Quelly, Mael MacMahon, Diogo Boil.[15]

The next event mentioned in the college records was the erratic behaviour of one of the students, Felix O'Neill, in 1631. He caused a stir by absenting himself from the college without permission and receiving and sending letters at various times without official sanction. An investigation was made into his lapses of obedience to the rules of the seminary. His fellow students were called into the presence of the rector to answer questions about the comings and goings of this student on 27 July 1631.[16]

Thanks to the investigation which was conducted with all the precision of a major event – with each student asked the same questions to which he was to answer 'yes' or 'no' with relevant details such as name, age and so forth being recorded. They are now of immense value as validating the presence of certain students in the college at the time.

There is no further information in the records about Felix being disciplined in any way. The incident seems to have been a storm in a teacup, and there does not appear to have been any serious misconduct on his part; it was perhaps a case of rebellion, secretive and disobedient behaviour in a strict college atmosphere. It is also recorded that he also missed lessons, had aggressive words with another collegian and threatened vengeance on him.

The students questioned were: Robert Plunket, who was a little less than 21 years on 27 July 1631, a native of Carristown, province of Ulster; Thomas Casey, under 26 years on 28 July 1631, a native of West Munster, city of Limerick; William Lombard, aged 18 years from the city of Wexford; and Edmund Murphy, 20 years, from Berehaven. Bernard Egan, Thomas Hagil (Hagie), Richard Fallon and Morgan Sheehy were also named without details of age or place of origin.[17]

14 Sal. Arch. 33/1/15.　**15** Sal. Arch. 33/1/14/15.　**16** Ibid.　**17** Sal. Arch. 33/1/15.

The students swore to tell the truth in reply to what they would be asked. There were six questions in all. Plunkett said he knew all the other collegians '*de trato y comunicacion con ellos*' (by talking and communication with them) for a little less that a year. He was asked if he knew that on the octave of Corpus Christi some of the students had gone out, '*sin licencia, a deshora y por puerta extraordinaria*' (without permission at an off time and by special exit). He replied that he had heard about it from themselves and that Felix had not come down to meditation with the others. He knew that another called Felix had gone out but he did not recall who. He knew that Felix had missed lessons against the orders of the superior and he knew that Felix had '*palabras graves*' (serious words) with another collegian and threatened him with vengeance. He knew that Felix sometimes went to the post office where he received and sent post without permission. He thought that Felix was friendly with Bernardo (Egan).

Thomas Casey, a priest, swore *in verbo sacerdotis* to tell the truth and the others answered in similar vein.

The third event of importance in the college in Santiago was the series of complaints sent in a memorial[18] to Philip IV by the students of all the Irish Colleges in Spain about the Jesuit administration of the colleges. They claim that the colleges could sustain more students than they did and often only accommodated half or less than that. Santiago is mentioned as being able to sustain 16 students. In 1633 there were no students in the college, in 1634 and 1635 there was only one and in 1638–9 there were eight. It was further claimed that many were admitted who had no intention of going on the mission in Ireland but rather wished to join the Society of Jesus. It was also alleged that children of tender age were admitted not because they were fit for the courses taught in the college but because they were related to Irish Jesuit fathers.[19]

Another point made was that there were on the staff fathers and lay brothers who were superfluous. It was also said that these were treated better than the collegians. The students also contended that the courses given in the college were not suitable for those who wished to go back to Ireland to preach and teach the faith, and complained that in Salamanca the theology course had been reduced to three years and in Santiago the arts course to two. They also asserted that if students are sent to the

Bernard Egan was considered to be a friend of Felix O'Neill. **18** Rivera, op. cit., pp 429–30. **19** One example is that of two nephews of Fr Luke Wadding, minors, who attended the college in 1623, Sal. Arch. 34/2, ff. 15 and 17.

university they were only allowed to attend lectures given by members of the Society and were prevented from graduating so that in Ireland they would not have any prestige or the possibility of attaining ecclesiastical dignities. The Jesuits have never wished to put libraries into the colleges and the students complain that books are in short supply. It was further claimed that they are prevented from communicating with Spaniards and from perfecting their knowledge of the Spanish language. This, they asserted, was so that they could not complain and hence were more strongly subject to the Jesuit fathers. It was certainly true that in Santiago they were prevented from doing any pastoral work, but the other accusations sound rather far-fetched.

The clothes given to them also come in for criticism. They did not provide good cover for them and lacked cleanliness and decency, and for the whole year they are given only one pair of hose and for underwear two shirts of coarse linen. The daily sustenence was limited and at times did not reach even what was absolutely necessary. There was excessive difference between the food that the Jesuits who live in the seminary received and what the seminarians got. The mutton which in the Jesuit houses was about to rot was usually sent to the seminaries, and the same happened with stale bread and rotten fruit. It is difficult to believe that this has any basis in fact, but there was evidently strong opposition to the Spanish Jesuit control of the college and the insistence by the Royal College that it had jurisdiction over the Irish College of Santiago de Compostela at that time.

The memorial claimed that there was great lack of care for the students and they were even manhandled, most of the time without any cause, but that they criticised the poor administration.

It was also claimed in this memorial that the fathers put great effort into opposing the liberty of the collegians. When the Marqués de Mancera, governor of Galicia from 1631 to 1638, heard that in the Santiago college there were not the numbers that could be sustained and of the ill-treatment of the few that were in it, he asked the fathers for an explananation of how the income was employed. As they did not give an explanation, the governor stopped the grant for a year and a half, and in consequence half of the collegians were sent away by the fathers.

Rivera points out that these strong complaints were probably exaggerated and unfair. It is possible that the Society had little interest or indeed it may even have felt great displeasure or resentment in the beginning at having been forced to take over the direction of the Irish seminaries in Spain by royal order, apparently against their will or better judgment.

It does appear, however, that Philip IV set up rules and a constitution in the Compostela college three years later. Efforts to get more authority for the rectors of the Santiago institution were strenuously made but were just as strenuously opposed by the provincials of the order. Naturally enough, the constitution was based on Jesuit norms and the general consensus was that the college was organised like a Jesuit novitiate, rather than as a college for training secular prists. However, it appears that after the introduction of the constitution the college became better organised and settled into a more peaceful mode.

Although the Sheehy episode took place in the Irish College, Salamanca in 1751, it impinges on the Irish College, Santiago, since five of the seminarians who were involved in it had studied in Santiago. They were John Coleman, Bernard Downes, Nicholas White, Thomas Kirwan and Nicholas Sheehy. They were all apparently very good students and were duly ordained to the priesthood. As already mentioned, it was customary before leaving the college to have clothes made by a tailor for each of them. These were lay clothes to conceal the fact on arrival in Ireland that they were priests. Each student was given a viaticum, about £10, for his journey home and to defray the cost of the clothing.

It appears that a travelling tailor, an old man, possibly Irish, had called to the college in Salamanca looking for work and the students asked the rector for permission to have him make their clothes. Rector O'Brien refused, saying that they did not know anything about this man. In defiance, the young clerics hid the tailor in the college, secretly fed him and engaged him to make the clothes. Eventually they were found out and the tailor was thrown out. The students reacted violently and there was an acrimonious conflict.

The rector waited five days to see if they would ask for pardon. They saw nothing wrong with what they did, so on the sixth day he deprived them of their breakfast. They 'tumultuosly and seditiously appealed to the Royal College who considered that the rector of the Irish College had not ordered disproportionate punishment and suggested that three should remain on their knees for a day in the refectory and the other should kiss the rector's feet. There was a wild uproar by the students; then they left the college.

Three of them were expelled – Kirwan, Sheehy and White – and the other two, Downes and Coleman, were sent away from the college without letters of recommendation. A very serious view was taken of their behaviour by the authorities in Salamanca, and also it seems by the church authorities in Ireland on their return.

Fr Ranson noted[20] that it is difficult to understand why they were hounded without let-up with much venom and bitterness when eventually they arrived back in Ireland. Various efforts were made on their behalf in Salamanca by numerous people and they were advised to apologise; but this advice was not heeded.

Apart from the students and rectors, many eminent Irish churchmen and others lived and died in Santiago. In addition there were many distinguished Spaniards who took part in the life of the college over its history. The included several governors of Galicia.

The governor of Galicia, the Conde de Caracena, Luís de Carillo de Toledo, lived in La Coruña. The Irish scholar, Patrick Sinnott, was tutor to his children and to the O'Sullivan children who lived in his house. Daniel O' Sullivan was sent there when he was five years of age. He was brought up as a member of the family and called the count and his wife 'father' and 'mother'.

Even though Caracena was transferred from Galicia to Valencia in 1606, he still continued to take an interest in the Irish. A couple of years after he left Galicia to take up his post, he obtained an order from the king that his successor would continue to see that the Irish College got the royal grant. Ever afterwards from time to time he begged the king to keep up the help to the Irish. He died in 1626.

The Marqués de Mancera, Pedro de Toledo y Leyra, was a governor of Galicia who died in 1652. He was *Teniente de las galeras del rey* and *Virrey del Peru* (lieutenant general of the king's galleys and the viceroy of Peru).

Admiral Diego de Brochero y Anaya, Prior of Ireland, the admiral who was in command of the naval side of the Armada which came to Kinsale, was also regarded as an influential friend and protector of the Irish. Another champion of the Irish was don Francisco Arias Dávila y Bobadilla, with the fierce-sounding title of Conde de Puñonrostro (the count of a fist in face). His secretary was a Kerryman, Maurice Cornelio.[21]

Another benefactor of the college was Sir William Godolphin (?–1696) an English MP, ambassador of King Charles II to Spain, Lord Privy Seal. Accused of conspiracy in the Popish Plot, he was dismissed in 1678, settled in Madrid and died there in 1696. He was a wealthy man, and a legacy of

---

20 Sal. Arch. II, 6, 7, 8 (1913); XIII, 52/1/2. **21** *Knights*, iv, p. 2.

3,000 *reales* was received by the Irish College at Santiago from his estate in 1697. He also left sums of money to other Irish Colleges.[22]

Francisco de Sandoval, Duque de Lerma, got political power under Philip III (1551–1625), who entrusted all authority to him as the royal favourite. He expelled the *moriscos*, the Moors, in 1616. He left the court in 1618 when he fell from power.

At least two Spaniards were appointed to bishoprics in Ireland. The most notable was Fray Mateo de Oviedo OFM, nominated archbishop of Dublin by the pope in 1599 at the behest of the Irish. He was a Castillian from Segovia, guardian of the monastery of San Francisco de Santiago. He became a strong supporter of the Irish cause and spent a considerable length of time in Ireland, and it is said that he knew the country, the people and even the language well. He was there during the Desmond guerilla war of 1580–3 against the English.

Another Spaniard, Francisco de Ribera OFM (1587–1604), who was based in the Low Countries, was nominated bishop of Kildare, but never came to Ireland.[23]

Several Irish bishops were appointed suffragans of the archbishop of Santiago. From time to time Irish prelates sought refuge in the kingdom of Galicia. In the later sixteenth century Peter Power or de la Poer, bishop of Ferns, was a suffragan. At a later stage it became the custom to appoint exiled bishops from Ireland who had found refuge in Galicia as suffragans. These included Thomas Strong, Ossory, Thomas Walsh, Cashel and Nicholas French, bishop of Ferns.

The bishops of Ferns had a special relationship with Spain and were especially favoured in this respect. Nicolas French (1646–78), bishop of Ferns, was driven out of Ireland in 1649. He lived in Santiago from 1659 until 1665. He left on 24 March 1665 and was in San Sebastian on 8 May with the intention of sailing to Ireland. He was in Bordeaux on 22 May 1665. The duke of Ormond prevented him from entering the country. He died at Ghent in 1678.

He rented a room in a house belonging to the Irish College in Santiago in 1662, at a rent of 250 *reales* and which he occupied for six months. He is also recorded as paying 100 *reales* for the same room for three months.[24]

Pedro Ruiz de los Santos, a grandnephew of Bishop French, was a candidate for a knighthood in 1668. He came to Spain from Ireland in 1631

22 Sal. Arch. 34/2, f. 115.   **23** Enrique Garcia Hernán, *Irlanda y el rey prudente*, ii, p. 130.   **24** Sal. Arch. 34/2, f. 65.

as a small child (he was 37 years old in 1668) with his parents and an older sister. Two years later Bishop Nicholas French, a brother of his grandmother (his mother is mentioned in the records but it has to be his grandmother), arrived in La Coruña. Pedro Ruiz de los Santos came to Vizcaya where they landed and then to San Lucar de Barrameda and lived there with his parents until the death of his father in 1647. His father was John de los Santos. His mother and sister died in the *peste* (plague) about 1649 when he was serving in Italy. His mother was Cathalina Ruiz and her mother was Elena Frens (French), sister of the bishop. His uncle, the bishop, was still alive and went to Lorena in France as ambassador of the Irish Catholics. He returned to Spain later and was made a co-adjutor to don Pedro de Carillo, archbishop of Santiago.

Among the sponsors for Pedro Ruiz de los Santos were Fr Dermot Fayo from Limerick city and Patrick Mulledy, member of the Spanish Council for Flanders and former Spanish ambassador to England. Two other sponsors were from Leinster, Patrick Hadsor from Co. Louth and Cornelio Suleban from Bearhaven, Co. Cork.[25]

Nicholas Sweetman, bishop of Ferns (1745–86), also studied in the Santiago college and returned to Ireland in 1724. He was exiled to Spain and was also auxiliary to the archbishop of Santiago.

Thomas Walsh (Valois) was born 1580. He was very ill and had to be carried from Clonmel to Waterford to be banished and shipped out of Ireland for Spain. He was archbishop of Cashel (1626–54), son of Robert Walsh and Anastasia Strong, born Waterford, diocese of Waterford and Lismore. He studied in the Irish College, Salamanca, was aged 22 in 1602, and died in the Irish College, Santiago in 1654. He made a will in Santiago in 1654 when William Salinger was rector of the Irish College. This fragile manuscript was witnessed by William Salinger. In it the archbishop left an amount of money to his church of St Patrick in Cashel, some for masses for his soul; two pontifical robes, one of white silk and the other of purple cloth, his chalices and books and his pectoral and ring were left to his successor.[26]

Bishop Walsh had been a merchant in Lisbon for two years before he entered St Patrick's college in Lisbon and later Salamanca. He was a priest in 1618 when he went back to Ireland.

25 *Knights*, iii, p. 13.   26 Sal. Arch., 35/2.

Thomas Strong, bishop of Ossory (1582–1602), arrived in Lisbon in 1581 and died in Santiago on 20 January 1602. He was also known as Philip Fitzthomas and was a suffragan to the archbishop of Santiago, Alonso Vazquez.[27] He also objected to the Jesuit take-over. He was an uncle of Thomas White SJ and was related to Dr Walsh, archbishop of Cashel, Nicholas Comerford SJ, Dr Comerford, bishop of Waterford, Fr Lombard SJ and Andrew Wise, Grand Prior of the order of Malta at Capua. He died in Santiago in 1602 and is buried in the cloister of the cathedral.

Florence Conry OFM was archbishop of Tuam. He was O'Neill's representative in Spain and accompanied Martin de la Cerda from La Coruña in 1603 when he was on a mission to Hugh O'Neill in Ireland. He was one of the main objectors to the Jesuit take-over of the Irish College, Santiago. He was a scholar who translated the popular Spanish devotional work, *El espejo de devoción*, into Irish as *Sgáthan an Chrábhaidh* in 1616.[28]

Many of the Irish Jesuits in Santiago produced learned works on theology and philosophy. They included Paul Sherlock, author of works on the Canticle of Canticles, already mentioned, and Richard Lynch, whose *Universa philosophia scholastica* was published in Lyon in 1654. In February 1678 Fr Patrick Lynch was lent 3,000 *reales* by Fr Andrew Lynch SJ, rector of the Santiago college, with the permission of the Provincial of Castile, Fr Geronimo, to assist the work he had in hands of the printing of the papers of Fr Richard Lynch SJ. The licence was given on condition that Fr Patrick Lynch was to pay half of the 3,000 *reales* after the printing and the other half the following year. Patrick Lynch agreed to these conditions and signed documents to this effect in the Jesuit college in Medina del Campo on 15 June 1678.[29]

Other Jesuits were teachers of philosophy or theology. For example, Thomas Comerford SJ taught philosophy in Santiago before 1617, John Egan SJ (born in 1594 and died in 1664) lived in Kilkenny in 1649 when he was 55 years of age. He studied philosophy and theology in Galicia. He returned to Ireland and taught philosophy there. He was exiled by Cromwell in 1652 and taught this subject in the Irish College, Santiago from 1663 until his death in 1664.

Intriguing personages of all kinds pass momentarily, often in a single reference, through the pages of the income and payments in the pages of

27 Castelao, op. cit., p. 95.   28 Penny Woods, 'Books rich and rare', p. 48.
29 Sal. Arch. 34/2, f. 105v, 112v.; P. Woods, 'Books rich and rare', p. 44.

the principal college ledger – Cardinal Roxano who donated four doubloons when he was present at a ceremony in the college *c.*1665, the Conde de Massada who gave 288 *reales* when he attended a ceremony *c.*1661, an archdeacon who gave a donation of 300 *reales*, an unnamed *capitán flamenco* who gave a *limosna* (alms) of 2 doubloons to the college in 1657 and an unnamed *Teniente General* who in 1714 paid for the *alimentos* (board) for his nephew, Dr Richard Fallon, canon of Murcia, who made contributions to the college from time to time and also left a legacy in his will to the college.

Many reports on Ireland were produced by Spaniards not only in the late sixteenth century and early seventeen century but in earlier centuries also. For example, the Catalan, Ramon de Parallos wrote a description of Irish customs in Ulster; its dress, food and drink are detailed in his work when he returned to Spain from Ireland in 1398. He compared Dublin, Drogheda and Dundalk with Spanish towns and was impressed with the countryside of Ulster. He even praised the good looks of men and women among O'Neill's followers. The great Franciscan preacher, Juan de Capistrano (1386–1456), also visited our island.[30]

Reports on Ireland were produced by Fernando de Barrionuevo, Martin de la Cerda, Diego Brochero, Vasco de Saavedra, Pedro de Sandobal, López de Soto and Fray Mateo himself. Before Kinsale there were, of course, many reports by those coming to survey the country prior to the invasion. Many secret agents spent time here and Spanish ambassadors in London (among them at this early stage there were Irish holders of this office, as were the chaplains to the embassy also) naturally sent reports back to Madrid. Spanish archives are rich in documentation as early as the thirteenth and fourteenth centuries.

---

30 Enrique García Hernán, op. cit., i, p. 12.

CHAPTER 7

Conclusion

It is difficult to assess the numbers of students who studied at the Irish College at Santiago de Compostela. I have listed just under 350 names in Chapter 5 for the period 1605–1769. Taking a very low average of four students each year would give a total of 535 over the life of the college, so my list must be considered a partial list of students of the Santiago college. In an examination of the available records I found no student numbers or names for some years. Apart from the names of the O'Sullivan Beare contingent I found no other names for the period 1605–13. Taking the period 1614–69, I found none for 1621–2; 1627–8; 1633; 1636; 1643; 1684–6; 1692–3; 1698–9; 1717; 1721; 1742; I found only one or two for the following years 1620; 1626[1]; 1629; 1634–5; 1637; 1642; 1652–5; 1680–3; 1687–1691; 1694; 1697; 1700–1; 1709; 1716; 1618; 1722; 1730; 1739; 1745; 1751; 1754; 1763; 1769. For the rest of the years there were numbers ranging from three to twelve per year, with fourteen in 1624 and sixteen in 1618 and 1649. Again it is difficult without exact dates to tell when a student went onto the roll in the college or when he left. The system for enrolment was that information was sent to Ireland when vacancies occurred. In accordance with the scheme for allocation of places, equal numbers were taken in from each ecclesiastical province. A diocese within that province was declared to be entitled to a vacancy. This was the theory but, naturally, it was not easy to coordinate arrivals and departures.

In general, the students came in the autumn to start their course and left in the summer, two years later, say for example, autumn 1650 to summer 1652. We can see from numerous examples, that this was not always strictly adhered to. The academic year ran from the feast of St Luke, 18 October, to that of St John, 24 June. It must be admitted that the course in the Santiago college was similar to an apprenticeship or a clearing house. The student spent two years there doing a mixed arts and

---

1 See Sal. Arch. 34/2, f. 20. According to this reference five unnamed students arrived in the Irish College, Santiago from Ireland sometime between 1626 and 1628.

philosophy course, and the real groundwork for him was the three years' study of theology in the Irish College at Salamanca.

In the Salamanca manuscripts there are many instances of details of the number of students arriving there from Santiago and very often giving their date of arrival. However, this is not always the case. For example, I found ten students in the college in Santiago in 1741 and none in 1742, presumably the ten had departed to Salamanca. However, there was no record of ten students arriving there in 1742; but the Salamanca records the following year, on 29 August 1743 showed seven students, identifiable as Santiago students, taking their first year examination in theology in Salamanca. A further check revealed that six of them took the oath in Salamanca in May 1742.[2]

Nicholas Morris could be taken as a typical example of a student who went through the system, according to the rules, from his two years' philosophy in Santiago and three years' theology in the Irish College, Salamanca until final ordination and return to his homeland. He came to Santiago, probably in September 1748, took his oath in March 1749 and probably finished his arts/philosophy course in June 1751. He took the oath in Salamanca on 13 September 1751, sat his first year examination in August 1752, his second in August 1753 and his third in June 1654. He was ordained three months before his final examination and returned to Ireland ten days after his final examination.[3]

In the early stages many students entered the Jesuit order and were in many cases lost to the Irish church. However, in the majority of cases the seminarians stayed the course for the secular priesthood; there were a few drop-outs; some found themselves unable to keep up with the course; others discovered that they had not a vocation and others had to leave for health reasons. Some joined the Franciscans, Augustinians or other religious orders. A few lingered in Spain, mainly as chaplains either to Irish regiments or to noble families. However, it is clear that the majority were ordained as secular priests and returned to Ireland to serve their people.

As I have already said, at a later stage it was thought by some opponents of the administration of the college by the Society of Jesus that the college was like a novitiate for the Jesuit Order. Certainly some of the students in the early years were related to members of the order and often to each other. Many of the prominent south Munster and south Leinster names such as Comerford, White, Walsh, Wadding, Shea, Garvey, Archer,

2 *Arch. Hib.* 4, pp 7, 29.   3 Sal. Arch. XXIII/1/ii; *Arch. Hib.* 4, pp 8, 36, 37.

Strong, Lombard, Dormer, Butler, Conroy and Carney did show up among the students and the ranks of the Jesuits, and certainly many of the early students were related to the early Jesuits and also in varying degrees to each other. There were also strong Waterford, Cashel and Clonmel connections with the college. Examples abound: the students John Conroy, son of Peter Conroy and Elizabeth Saul, and the two brothers, James and John Carney, sons of Philip Carney and Helen Saul. Both their mothers bore the maiden name Saul, and were probably sisters or cousins. They were all from the archdiocese of Cashel and were in the Irish College, Santiago at the same time, prior to 1618.

Details of the place of birth of only a small number of students are to be found in the records. One may hazard a guess, for instance, that a Kirwan usually came from Galway, a Butler from Kilkenny and a Barry from Cork. The earliest students clearly came from O'Sullivan Beare country, and there were MacCarthys, O'Sullivans, O'Driscoll, with a smattering of Fitzgeralds (Geraldines), Sinnotts and others from the dioceses of Ardfert, Ross, Cork and Cloyne. Some others came from Waterford, Meath, Dublin, Ferns, Ossory, Cashel and Kilmore.

In addition to the seminarians in the college in Santiago there are names of Irish and Spanish students, who also attended the college. These were probably not clerical students. In some cases they are clearly boarders or *convictores* who may have been taken on to help finances. The Irish were undoubtedly sons or nephews of Irish residents in Galicia or were enrolled because they were related to some of the Jesuit fathers who, like the Irish residents, paid for their board and lodging.

One student of special interest in the later category was Nicholas Stafford. He was from La Coruña, son of Philip and Catalina Stafford of that city. Philip Stafford has already been mentioned as consul for England and Ireland in La Coruña, and has been noted regarding some dealings with the college. Nicholas was born on 27 January 1663, he was received into the Society of Jesus on 28 March 1680 and completed his noviceship in the Irish College Santiago de Compostela. He was ordained c.1686 and was sent to serve in his native city of La Coruña. He died aged 33 years on 10 August 1695.

Some of the Spaniards who stayed in the college from time to time appear to have been young boarders of school age. In some cases they were accompanied by one or two servants and occasionally by their tutors. Anyone familiar with the picaresque novels in Spain will know that students as well as scholboys in the sixteenth and seventeenth centuries were often accompanied by their servants when at school or college, as were blind beggars, clerics, poor squires and the many other vagabonds who roamed the roads of Spain.[4]

It appears that the practice of taking in Spanish boarders in Santiago gave rise to criticism from a least one other Irish College. The rector of the Irish College, Salamanca, Dr John O'Brien, a Waterford man (1743–60), was scathing about the practice. Ironically, this was when he himself wished to take in two young boarders in Salamanca. They were nephews of an important nobleman, the Marqués de la Cañada, an expatriate Irishman domiciled in Cadiz, named Juan Batista Terry. The young men were Patricio and Pedro Terry, the sons of his brother, Pedro Terry, who was a member of the Council of the High Audit of Madrid.

In his *Diario*, rector O'Brien notes that 'the rules of the seminary allowed the reception of Irish nationals of distinction, and that by this precedent the door will not be opened, as in Santiago, for sons of Spaniards because this is not the same.'[5]

The Irish were identified with most of the Catholic enemies of England. Hugh O Neill certainly identified his struggle against the English crown with the defence of Catholicism against the inroads of the Reformation thereby persuading the pope and the king of Spain to recognise the Irish struggle as a Catholic crusade or war.

It has been pointed out by Burrieza[6] that there was some concern in the kingdom of Spain that '*bajo el disfrazado marco del exilio catolíco, se introdujes la herejía en Castilla*' (under the guise of Catholic exile heresy might be introduced into Castile).

The Irish emigré population in the sixteenth and seventeen centuries in France, Spain and Portugal were closely watched and the colleges came in for special attention from the numerous spies planted at continental ports and known to ingratiate themselves with the exiled students and clerics.

---

4 See *Lazarillo de Tormes*, the most famous of the picaresque novels. It was published anonymously in Alcalá de Henares, Burgos and Antwerp in 1554. Others were Alemán's *Guzman de Alfarache; La vida del escudero Marcos de Obregón* by Vicente Espinel; and Francisco de Quevedo's *La vida del buscón* (1626). The genre was imitated all over Spain and in other countries, and the best examples were translated into many languages.   5 D. O'Doherty, Arch. Hib. 4 (1915), pp 32–3.   6 Javier Burrieza Sanchez, '*Escuelas de sacerdotes y mártires : los colegios del exilio católico*' in Enrique García-Hernán et al. (eds), *Irlanda y la monarquía hispánica Kinsale, 1601–2001 Guerra, política, exilio y relegación* (Madrid, 2002) p. 41.

The Calendars of State Papers and other sources such as the Public Record Office in London attest to this. So, the exiles were forced to use elaborate subterfuges. As letters were quite often confiscated, intercepted or opened by the authorities, the exiled students in writing home frequently used their mothers' maiden names; a Jesuit Fr St Leger used his mother's name Gough, another, Fr Charles Leae, whose father was Morris, or Muiris, used the name McMorris, to put the spies off the scent.

Aliases, often several different ones, were employed especially by the Jesuits. These were easily formed, especially easy with Irish surnames, with the several additions of Mac (son of) the Irish custom of changing the name in each generation; i.e. John MacMorris could eventually become MacSean (or MacJohn) of even FitzJohn and so on. Fr James Archer SJ (1537–1677) often became James Bowman when he came back to Ireland. So the exiles were forced to use subterfuges and going down the line with each generation with Mac a man could distance himself from the current English form of his name, since the English surname used only one patronymic.

Paul Sherlock in his work on the Canticle of Canticles used his mother's maiden name, Leonard, as author of the second volume. This may or may not have been also because he had been attacked by an Italian cleric in his interpretation. But generally the use of the mother's name was to hide the identity of the user. The outlawed priests travelling back and forth to the continent and posing as merchants had to learn to be very devious in their dealings with the powerful who ruled Ireland at that time. Priests adopted many disguises also, some very colourful. One such priest had disguised himself as a Walloon merchant but aroused suspicion because, as the spy reported to his masters, he did not appear to be carrying samples of the merchandise that he was suposed to be dealing in.[7]

The spies were an unsavoury lot, and there are many cases of their reports being a tissue of lies. For example, the case of the Irish College at Bordeaux in France comes to mind. It was reported as a hotbed of treason. Lisbon was given a similar description. Indeed, a copy of Dermot MacCarthy's list of priests expelled from Ireland[8] and who were living in Bordeaux found its way by some devious means into the Calendar of State

---

7 Professor P. Corish has written interesting descriptions of the deceptions practised. See P. Corish in *Arch. Hib.* 27 (1964), p. 87 and Karen Harvey, op. cit., pp 98–9.   **8** He was the rector and founder of the Irish College in Bordeaux.

Papers. There was money to be made if the story was lurid enough, and informants had vivid imaginations. Suffice to say that at the time if a priest was disovered in Ireland by a priest-hunter, the reward was £30; and a Jesuit was an even bigger fish netting a reward of £50.

Another example is the fact that the letters from Irish priests in the Irish College, Lisbon regarding the opening ceremonies of the college there in 1590 are to be found in the British Museum. They were seized by the skipper of an English pirate ship operating out of Bristol who had boarded and sacked a merchant ship off the Portuguese coast. This ship was carrying mail from Lisbon to a port near Santiago de Compostela. The letters were retained and handed over to the mayor of Bristol and eventually ended up in the British Museum.

The history of the exiled seminaries and the Irish College movement in Europe is an inspiring human saga. After a long period of study abroad the newly trained priests returned to a land where life was harsh, difficult, uncertain and often dangerous.

The colleges under the control of the Jesuits played a decisive role in the consolidation of the Counter-Reformation in Ireland even though at one remove from the country and planned in another kingdom. Various elements combined to make it fraught with difficulties: there were divisions between the seculars and the regulars (or order priests), between Jesuits, Franciscans, Dominicans, between the Old English and the Old Irish and recent immigrants and those of longer standing. Through the control of the Irish Colleges the Jesuits exercised in the early seventeenth century a huge importance in the reorganisation of the church in Ireland. This included the setting up of spiritual, theological and cultural elements which moulded the early modern Irish Catholic church and has not as yet been sufficiently studied.[9]

Undoubtedly, the majority of the secular priests trained on the continent for the Irish mission came from the larger colleges, but the smaller colleges also sent significant numbers throughout all the time that they operated in Spain. Also, after Kinsale Spain's peace with England gave that kingdom many problems juggling her foreign policy: she had to maintain peace with England while at the same time support the Irish church outlawed by the English and which she was helping to function underground. But then we must remember that at the same time the

9 Some recent work by Dr Declan Downey is now emphasising this theme. See the Bibliography for details.

Dutch rebels were receiving support from England against Spain in the Low Countries.

The Irish Colleges in Spain were part of the Spanish response to the consequences of the unsuccessful military expedition to Ireland. Their foundation marks less a new phase in Hiberno-Spanish relations than a new phase in the Habsburg grand strategy, which from 1604 included peace with England, as I have already pointed out.

The colleges operated as part of the Irish Catholic *natio*. They functioned to produce priests for the Irish church, helped train others for professional activity in Ireland and elsewhere, and acted as social and political centres for expatriate Irish communities in Spain. Whether or not any of the Spanish colleges assumed the importance among the local Irish communities which the Paris college, for example, achieved for the Parisian Irish is difficult to say. It appears that the importance of the Spanish colleges lessened in the seventeenth and eighteenth centuries. Spain's political star waned, Irish migration to Spain declined, local Irish communities became thoroughly integrated into Spanish life, the Catholics in Penal Ireland grew better organised, and France rose to prominence.

Further research will help us to establish links between the merchant and military communities on the one hand and the students of the colleges on the other.[10] It will also provide us with a clearer idea of the academic curricula in the colleges.

My work on this college and those associated with it is at this stage in essence a pioneering operation. The process has three layers – identification, place of birth and eventual place or places of ministry. Further research will assuredly elicit more information about those students and in some cases rectors and other associated figures who are presented with only a name and date. Because for obvious reasons there is a dearth of church archives in Ireland in the time of the Reformation and subsequent centuries, we have to follow the careers of these priests mainly in continental sources. My hope is to fill in and flesh out these spectral figures from the past by tracking their lives and finding their rightful places in the history of the Irish church and its neglected clerical personages of the late

---

10 See Karen Harvey, op. cit., pp 82–92; J.J. Simms, 'The Irish on the Continent 1691–1800', in Moody et al. (eds), *New history of Ireland*, iv p. 639; Harmon Murtagh, 'Irish soldiers abroad 1600–1800' in Thomas Bartlett and Keith Jeffrey (eds), *A military history of Ireland* (Cambridge, 1996), p. 298; John C. O'Callaghan, *History of the Irish Brigades in the service of France* (Glasgow, 1870).

sixteenth, seventeenth and eighteenth centuries, for most of whom records exist only in continental archives. In spite of the enormous difficulties I am optimistic that this will be possible.

The suppression of the Jesuits, the French Revolution and the founding of Maynooth in 1795 were the three decisive blows to the continental college network. The loss of the continental connection which had shaped the Irish Catholic ethos for a long time is to be regretted and possibly led to unnecessary standardisation in the training of clerical students in Ireland.

Bibliography

Act for the registration of popish clergy 1703.

Arnáiz, María-José, and José Luís Sánchez, *El colegio de los irlandeses* (Alcalá/Madrid, 1985).

Bartlett, Thomas, & Keith Jeffrey (eds), *A military history of Ireland* (Cambridge, 1996).

Begley, G., *The diocese of Limerick from 1691 to the present time* (Dublin, 1938).

Boyle, Patrick, *The Irish College in Paris* (Dublin, 1901).

Brady, John, & Patrick Corish, 'The church under the Penal Code' in *A history of Irish Catholicism*, iv (Dublin, 1971).

Brady, W. Maziere, *The episcopal succession in England, Scotland and Ireland, AD 1400–1875*, 2 volumes (Rome, 1876).

Byrne, Matthew J. Translation into English of part of *Historiae Catholicae Iberniae compendium* of Philip O'Sullivan Beare under the title, *Ireland under Elizabeth* … (Dublin, 1903).

Cabeza de Leon, S., *Historia de la universidad de Santiago* (Santiago, 1956).

Carrigan, William, *The history and antiquities of the diocese of Ossory*, 4 vols (Dublin, 1905)

Chambers, Ann, *At arm's length* (Dublin, 2004).

Cogan, A., *The ecclesiastical history of the diocese of Meath*, 3 vols (Dublin, 1867).

Comerford, D., *Collections relating to the diocese of Kildare and Leighlin*, 3 vols (Dublin, 1830).

Connell, Paul, 'Index of priests of the Meath diocese 1704–1993,' in O. Cavran (ed.), *History of the diocese of Meath 1860–1993*, 3 vols.

Corish, Patrick, 'Correspondence of the superior of the Jesuit mission in Ireland with John O'Brien, SJ, rector Salamanca', *Arch. Hib.* 27 (1964), pp 85–103.

Corkery, Daniel, *The fortunes of the Irish language* (Dublin, 1954).

——, *The hidden Ireland: a study of Gaelic Munster in the eighteenth century* (Dublin, 1967).

Cortes Vázquez, Luís, *La vida estudiantil en la Salamanca clásica* (Salamanca, 1996).

Couselo Bouzas, José, *El colegio de irlandeses de Santiago de Compostela* (Santiago, 1935).

Davies, Gareth A., 'The Irish College at Santiago de Compostela. Two documents about its early days' in Margaret Rees (ed.), *Catholic tastes and times: essays in honour of M.E. Williams* (Leeds, 1887), pp 81–126.

Davies, R. Trevor, *The Golden Age of Spain, 1501–1621* (London, 1935).

Donnelly, N., *A short history of some Dublin parishes* (Dublin, 1911).

Downey, Declan M., 'Irish-European Integration: the legacy of Charles V', in Judith Devlin & Howard B. Clarke (eds), *European encounters: essays in memory of Albert Lovett* (Dublin, 2003), pp 97–117.

——, 'Purity of blood and purity of faith in early modern Ireland', in Alan Ford and John McCafferty (eds), *The origins of sectarianism in modern Ireland* (Cambridge, 2005), pp 216–28.

——, 'A Castilian-Royalist cradling: Spanish-Habsburg formation of the early Irish Counter-Reformation', in H.B. Clarke & J.R.S. Phillips (eds), *Ireland, England and the Continent: essays in memory of a turbulent friar, F.X. Martin, OSA* (Dublin, 2006) pp 296–306.

Edwards, D., *Church and State in Tudor Ireland* (Dublin, 1935).

Espasa Calpe, *Enciclopedia universal ilustrada*, 40 volumes (Madrid, 1958).

Fagan, Patrick, *Divided loyalties: the question of the oath for Irish Catholics in the eighteenth century* (Dublin, 1997).

Finnegan, Francis, 'Biographical dictionary of Irish Jesuits in the times of the Society's third Irish mission 1598–1773' (unpublished)

Flood, J.M., *Ireland: its saints and scholars* (Dublin, n.d.).

Giblin, Cathaldus, OFM, 'Irish exiles in Catholic Europe' Part 3 in *A history of Irish Catholicism*, John Brady and Patrick Corish (eds), *The church under the Penal Code* (Dublin, 1971)

Hamilton, Aidan OSB, *The chronicles of the English Augustinian canonesses regular of the Latern at St Monica's in Louvain*, v. 1 (Edinburgh, 1904).

Harvey, Karen, *The Bellews of Mount Bellew* (Dublin, 1998).

Hogan, Edmund, SJ, *Distinguished Irishmen of the sixteenth century* (London, 1894).

Kagan, R.L., *Students and society in early modern Spain* (Baltimore and London, 1974).

Kamen, Henry, *The war of the Spanish succession in Spain* (London, 1969).

——, *Spain in the later seventeenth century* (London, 1983).

——, *Spain, 1469–1714* (London, 1991).

Kelly, Matthew, Modern text of Philip O'Sullivan Beares, *Historiae Catholicae Iberniae compendium* (Dublin, 1850).

Lennon, Colm, *Archbishop Richard Creagh of Armagh, 1523–86* (Dublin, 2000).

Lynch, John, *Spain under the Habsburgs, 1516–1598*, 2 vols (Oxford 1963–9).

——, *Bourbon Spain, 1700–1808* (Oxford, 1989).

McDonald, William, 'Irish ecclesiastical colleges since the reformation – Santiago', *IER*, 10 (1873–4), pp 196–211, 11 (1874), pp 113–14.

MacKiernan, Francis J., *Diocese of Kilmore: bishops, priests, 1136–1988* (Cavan, 1990).

MacRedmond, Louis, *To the greater glory: a history of the Irish Jesuits* (Dublin, 1991).

Moody, T.W. et al. (eds), *A new history of Ireland* (Oxford, 1976).

Moran, P.F., *Spicilegium Ossoriense*, 1 (Dublin, 1874)

Murphy, D., *Our martyrs, 1535–1691* (Dublin, 1896).

Neligan, Agnes (ed.), *Maynooth Library treasures* (Dublin, 1995).

O'Boyle, James, SJ, *The Irish Colleges on the continent: their origin and history* (Belfast, 1935).

O'Callaghan, John Cornelius, *History of the Irish Brigades in the service of France* (Glasgow, 1870).

O Connell, Patricia, *The Irish College at Alcalá de Henares, 1649–1785* (Dublin, 1997).

——, *The Irish College at Lisbon, 1590–1834* (Dublin, 2001)

——, 'The northern dioceses and the Irish College of Alcalá, Spain', *Ulster Local Studies* 15:2 (winter 1993).

——, 'Francisco de Quevedo's study of philosophy in the University of Alcalá de Henares', *Bulletin of Hispanic Studies* 49:3 (1972), pp 256–64.

——, 'The rectors and students of the Irish College at Alcalá de Henares Spain 1649–1785', *Sea. AM* 17:1 (1996–7), pp 77–88.

O'Connell, Philip, *The diocese of Kilmore: its history and antiquities* (Dublin, 1937).

O'Doherty, Denis J., 'Domnal O'Sullivan Beare and his family in Spain', *Studies*, 19 (1930), pp 211–26.

——, 'Students of the Irish Colleges,' *Arch. Hib.* 2 (1913), pp 1–36; 3 (1914), pp 87–112, 4 (1915), pp 1–58.

O'Donoghue, Fergus, SJ, 'The Jesuit Mission in Ireland, 1598–1651' (unpublished PhD thesis, Catholic University of America, Washington, DC, 1981).

O'Hanlon, Canon John, *History of the Queen's County*, 2 vols (Dublin, 1907 and 1914).

O Súilleabháin, Amhlaoibh (Humphrey O'Sullivan), *Cín Lae Amhlaoibh,* ed. Tomás de Bhaldraithe (Baile Atha Cliath, 1970).

O'Sullivan Beare, Philip, *Historiae Catholicae Iberniae compendium* (Lisbon, 1621).

Parker, Geoffrey, *The grand strategy of Philip II* (London, 1998).

——, *The army of Flanders and the Spanish Road, 1567–1659* (Cambridge, 1972 & 2004).

Richardson, Regina Whelan, 'The Salamanca Archives', in Agnes Neligan (ed.), *Maynooth Library treasures* (Dublin, 1995).

Rivera Vázquez, E., *Galicia, los jesuitas, sus colegios y enseñanza en los siglos XVI al XVIII* (Santiago, 1989).

Silke, Revd John J., *Kinsale: the Spanish intervention in Ireland at the end of the Elizabethan wars* (Liverpool, 1970).

Simms, J.J., 'The Irish on the continent 16918', in *New history of Ireland,* iv (Oxford, 1976).

Wall, Maureen, *The Penal Laws, 1691–1766* (Dublin, 1951).

Walsh, Micheline Kerney, *Spanish knights of Irish origins,* 4 vols (Dublin 1960, 1965, 1970 and 1978).

——, 'The Irish College, Alcalá de Henares', *Sea. AM,* 11:2 (1985).

——, *Destruction by peace: Hugh O'Neill after Kinsale* (Armagh, 1986).

Walsh, T.J., *The Irish continental college movement* (Cork, 1973).

Index